Sister to Sister

Dr. Marla Bennett

*For Angela —
Many Blessings
Dr. Marla Bennett*

Sister to Sister

Copyright @ 2020 Marla Bennett

All rights reserved. No part of this publication may be reproduced, stored in a retrieval system or transmitted in any form by any means, electronic, mechanical, photocopy, recording, or otherwise, except as provided by USA copyright law.

Printed in the United States of America

Scriptures noted (KJV) are taken from the King James Version of the Bible.

FOREWORD

Years ago, I took part in a Christmas project led by our pastor's wife, a wonderful, Spirit-filled woman of God. We were encouraged to pray over the names of a few women from a local women's recovery ministry and to write words of encouragement for them in blank journals that would be gifted to them as part of our Christmas banquet. I loved this idea and felt inspired by the Holy Spirit every time I sat down to write in these journals. I really wanted to bless and encourage these women as they journeyed down their newly found paths with Christ. When the day came to present the journals to the ladies, they all immediately opened them and began reading them. Of course, I watched for "my" ladies, but I didn't see what I expected. After reading the entries, many of them began weeping openly and holding one another. My pastor came over to me, and said, "Aren't those the journals you wrote?" I nodded. "God is really touching them through your words." Tears filled my eyes as I felt the Holy Spirit at work.

The next week, the Lord spoke to my heart. I felt Him calling me to encourage all of my sisters by writing a devotional. That week began my own, new journey of obedience. I hope you are inspired, encouraged, and challenged by the following words, dear sister. This book is for you.

ACKNOWLEDGEMENTS

Many people have helped me with this endeavor, but I would like to say a special thank you to those who went above and beyond in their support regarding this project.

First, I appreciate the prayer, encouragement, guidance, protection, and stellar editing skills of my husband. There is no way I could have accomplished this without you, Tim Bennett. You are the love of my life, and I am so grateful for you. Second, there is a group of sisters who has continually saturated me with prayer and encouragement from the beginning to the end of this project. Thank you, Sandra Garner, Cindy Smith, and Nikki Boutwell. I love you and appreciate you more than you will ever know. Last, I would like to thank Susie Jones, who was led by the Holy Spirit to give personalized journals to the women of the Butterfly Ranch years ago. I never would have been inspired to write this devotional if you hadn't shown me how my writing could make such a positive impact.

TABLE OF CONTENTS

Contents

- PRAISE AND WORSHIP 1
- RELATIONSHIPS 12
- FAITH AND MIRACLES 52
- VICTORY 67
- PEACE 86
- ENCOURAGEMENT 104
- EVANGELISM 115
- FORGIVENESS 130
- ABOUT THE AUTHOR 137

PRAISE AND WORSHIP

Dear Sister,

Today I am reminded of one sister's act of true, sacrificial worship. Her name was Mary, and her story is found in the twelfth chapter of John. Jesus traveled to Bethany to visit Lazarus and his family. This was the same Lazarus whom Jesus raised from the dead. Mary served the dinner, and Lazarus sat at the table with Jesus, but Mary humbled herself at Jesus' feet. She gave the only precious thing she owned, an alabaster box filled with expensive perfume. She bent down before Him, weeping so much that her tears bathed his feet, and poured her precious offering of worship over his skin. She used her own hair to dry the feet of Jesus.

Verse three says "Then took Mary a pound of ointment of spikenard, very costly, and anointed the feet of Jesus, and wiped his feet with her hair: and the house was filled with the odor of the ointment" (KJV).

There is so much sweet worship in this passage that it moves me to tears. In the midst of Martha serving the Lord and Lazarus supping with the Lord, Mary knelt and worshipped the Lord. She gave all she had with all of her heart. Her sacrificial worship filled the house with as much sweet aroma as did that expensive perfume. I Corinthians 11:15 says that a woman's hair is her glory, so Mary used her own glory to wipe the feet of Jesus. Her glory meant nothing to her compared to the Savior. Everyone who was in that house was touched by this act of worship. Everyone could tell that Mary gave her best to Jesus because the "house was filled with the odor." Mary entered that house smelling of sin and shame, but she rose from the feet of Jesus smelling like salvation and redemption, truly a delightful fragrance! Of course, as is the way of flesh and blood, as soon as Judas noticed what Mary had done, he began criticizing her.

      You know, sometimes people cannot stand to see someone truly worshipping the Lord. They feel they must criticize the worshipper, maybe saying "She's not really in the Spirit! Look how she's raising her hands. What a spectacle she is making of herself! She wouldn't be acting that way if it were really the Lord!" People with hard and jealous hearts can't stand to see true, abandoned worship and praise. However, no sooner had the critical words left Judas' mouth, that Jesus rose to Mary's defense. In verse seven, Jesus said "Let her alone; against the day of my burying hath she kept this" (KJV). Let me encourage you, dear sister, to worship Jesus with your all. Don't worry about those who might criticize you. Jesus will take care of them, and you won't have to do a thing!

Today's Prayer:

Dear Lord,

Help me to empty myself to you in worship today. Let me abandon all inhibitions and worries and lift my hands and voice in Your honor. I give my all to You, Jesus. All of my accomplishments are nothing when compared with Your magnificence. You are worthy of my worship. You are worthy of my praise. I empty my alabaster box at Your feet, Lord. Let the fragrance of Your worship fill my house, my workplace, my car, and my church. Let everyone around me automatically know that I worship an awesome God because of the sweet fragrance of worship that surrounds me.

In Jesus' Name,

Amen

Reflection:

What are your thoughts about today's devotional? What can you do to actively apply these principles?

Dear Sister,

I John 4:18 says "There is no fear in love; but perfect love casteth out fear: because fear hath torment." In other words, fear causes suffering, and suffering comes in so many different shapes and sizes. For example, anger has its roots in fear. Someone who is angry all the time often strikes out at others or himself. Why is this person so angry? Maybe he or she is angry because of the fear of not getting a desire fulfilled or maybe fear that a loved one will be overlooked, slighted, or hurt. Sometimes a person lashes out because of the fear of others getting too close or intimate, which can be scary. It can be because that angry person associates anger with power or control. No matter why, this type of fear is destructive and causes suffering all around.

Another type of fear is that which is directed within a person, like an anxiety attack. Often this type of fear mimics a heart attack with chest pain, sweating, the feeling of suffocation, and general disorientation. All of these experiences are based on lies. He or she is not having a heart attack, but it is certain that this person is suffering. Praise God for the rest of this verse: "Perfect love casteth out fear." Of course, Jesus is the embodiment of perfect love, and He is the Truth, the Way, and the Life. It is through Jesus that we can find perfect peace and a release of all our fear.

However, when we are in the middle of a trial caused by fear, what can we do at that moment? Another word for "love" is "worship." One sure way to cast fear out of our lives is by worshipping, right then and there. As odd as that sounds, if we take a minute and focus our attention on Jesus and start worshipping Him, adoring Him, singing about Him, loving Him, fear HAS to leave. Fear and Jesus cannot exist at the same time. Jesus will always win over fear. How do we get Jesus into our fearful situation? Through worship.

Today's Prayer:

Dear Lord,

 Help me to worship You no matter what trials or circumstances I encounter. Help me to adore You and sing Your praises whenever I am afraid of what is going on in my life. Help me to cast my cares on You and allow You to cast out all my anger, disappointment, and fear. I ask that You give me a deeper revelation of Your love and power, so I can worship you more instantly and more often with more confidence.

In Jesus' Name,

Amen

Reflection:

 What are your thoughts about today's devotional? What can you do to actively apply these principles?

Dear Sister,

Today I am reminded of the story about how God delivered the Children of Israel from Pharoah's army at the Red Sea. Right after the enemy's army was drowned in the waters, Miriam led the people in a song of praise: "And Miriam the prophetess, the sister of Aaron, took a timbrel in her hand; and all the women went out after her with timbrels and with dances. And Miriam answered them: 'Sing ye to the Lord, for He hath triumphed gloriously; the horse and his rider hath He thrown into the sea!'" This is from Exodus 15:20-21 (KJV).

It is so important to praise the Lord when He gives us victory, and it is proper for a woman to lead this praise. Some people think that women should be silent and let men do all the leading, but I am here to tell you that your voice is just as powerful as any man's voice! When you lift your voice up in praise, others will naturally want to follow suit! Look at Miriam! She led the entire population of Israel in a song of praise and worship! Don't let anyone try to stifle your voice! It is powerful in the Lord Jesus our Savior!

Today's Prayer:

Dear Lord,

Thank you for filling my mouth with a voice of praise! Help me not to limit my praise because of worldly rules and religious regulations. You are worthy of my praise, so help me not to hold back! Help me to lead others, men, women, and children, in songs of Your praise and victory! Let Your power be evident in all the words that I sing for Your glory!

In Jesus' Name,

Amen

Reflection:

What are your thoughts about today's devotional? What can you do to actively apply these principles?

Dear Sister,

Today I am reminded of the scripture that says "And when he had consulted with the people, he appointed singers unto the LORD, and that should praise the beauty of holiness, as they went out before the army, and to say, Praise the LORD; for his mercy endureth forever." This passage is from II Chronicles 20:21.

I love this story because it demonstrates the power of praising the Lord in the midst of our battles. Whenever we come into conflict, our first instinct should be to praise Jesus! In this scripture, the king sent the singers in FRONT of the army, singing all about the wonderful attributes of God and how the victory was already theirs! Praise God! Later on in that same spot, we read that the praise actually confused the enemy so much that they turned on each other and killed one another before God's people even entered the fight. What a testimony! We know that God already has won our battles before we ever land the first blow. All we must do is to remember to praise Him FIRST!

Today's Prayer:

Dear Lord,

Fill my mouth with Your praises today and every day! When people confront me, let Your praise be on my lips. When conflicts occur, let me sing Hallelujah! Let my mind and voice be so filled with Your praise and worship that all who would try to harm me will be so confused that they run away from me in seven different directions! You are worthy of my praise, and I honor You, Lord Jesus, for Your mercy endureth forever!

In Jesus' Name

Amen

Reflection:

What are your thoughts about today's devotional? What can you do to actively apply these principles?

Dear Sister,

Today, I am reminded of the scripture that says, "This is the day that the Lord has made. I will be glad and rejoice in it." This passage is from Psalm 118:24. I think this means that every day, we must make the choice to rejoice in what God has given us. Let's be honest. Some days are better than others. Sometimes we are struggling with depression, angry people, or personal loss. However, we must choose to rejoice in spite of our circumstances because God is good to us and has given us so much to be happy about. After all, every day of life gives us another opportunity to succeed, honor, and glorify the Lord!

Today's Prayer:
Dear Lord,

Help me to make the right choices today. Help me to praise You for all You have done and will do in my life. Today, no matter what, let Your praises fill my mouth. Help my life and my attitude honor and glorify you.
In Jesus' Name,
Amen

Reflection:

What are your thoughts about today's devotional? What can you do to actively apply these principles?

RELATIONSHIPS

Dear Sister,

    Today I am reminded of the scripture in Luke 6, where Jesus teaches us how to love. Have you ever met someone who just grated against your nerves or worked with someone whose personality conflicted with yours? Have you ever had to serve someone who was ungrateful or even rude to you for no reason at all? Sometimes people accidentally hurt our feelings, and then there are people who are intentionally and habitually hurtful. Jesus says we should "love [our] enemies" in verse 35 (KJV), but how are we supposed to love these people if we don't even like them? These are real world issues. However, it is through this act of love that the world will know we are truly Christians.

    I was once rude to a wonderful Christian man. I was far away from God at the time, and I had had some bad experiences with judgmental Christians. This man was working as a security guard for the college where I worked. He was clearly serving the Lord, and he was very kind to me, often escorting me out to my car because I worked until well after midnight. He would speak of God and his family to me, but I would blow cigarette smoke at him and freely curse around him. I figured he would "judge" me soon enough and I would be rid of him and his testifying. I was wrong. He kept checking on me and speaking with me, and when I looked into his eyes, I didn't see any judgement. I only saw the love of Jesus.

Before long, I began confiding in him about my experiences with religion, and he listened patiently and gave good advice. It was this calm, steady, and sincere love that ushered me back into the arms of a loving God. I will forever be grateful that he looked through my rude and worldly behavior and saw a hurting soul. Jesus says in verse 35 that loving our enemies is what makes us "the children of the Highest." The next time someone is hateful to you, make the choice to intentionally love him or her. Remember that Jesus loved us when we were unlovely. Let's take the opportunity to be Jesus to all those around us today.

Today's prayer:

Dear Lord,

Lead me to people who are rude, hateful, and sinful. Help me to lead them to You by showing the love and acceptance of Christ. Don't let me fall into the temptation of responding with judgment or self-righteousness. Keep my eye on the goal of winning souls for Christ. Give me the words of love and wisdom that will break their hearts free from condemnation and lead them into the Kingdom of Heaven!

Reflection:

What are your thoughts about today's devotional? What can you do to actively apply these principles?

Dear Sister,

Today I am reminded of the scripture in Exodus 34, when Moses came down from Mount Sinai. God had called Moses up to the mountain to spend 40 days and 40 nights fasting in His presence. It was during this time that God shared His covenant with the children of Israel through His ten commandments. Moses heard the voice of God, and climbed the holy mountain. Later, he received the commandments and returned to his people, but he had been drastically changed. Verse 29 says, "Moses came down from Mount Sinai with the two tables of testimony in Moses' hand… [and]…wist not that the skin of his face shone while he talked with him" (KJV). He had been in the prolonged presence of God, and it showed. His face shined in a supernatural way, but he didn't even realize it. His face was so bright that his own brother, Aaron, and all of the people of Israel were frightened of him and ran away. Moses had to call them back to give them the message God had given him. Thereafter, his face shined so much that he had to wear a veil to put the people at ease.

Have you ever known someone who has spent a lot of time with God through fasting, prayer, praise, and worship? They are drastically and noticeably different. They don't look or act the same as everyone else, and sometimes people are convicted just by being in their presence. You cannot spend that kind of time with God and NOT be changed. It is the nature of God to change whomever or whatever He contacts. In the beginning, the world was without shape, but with God's contact, it became the beautiful earth we live in now.

When we first come to God, we are sinners, lost and without hope, but one moment in His presence of forgiveness makes us new creatures with a promise of everlasting life! God wants to spend time with us. He wants to transform us. He wants to make us vessels of His shining glory. The only way that can happen is if we make it a priority to spend time with Him. There will always be chores, duties, jobs, to distract us. However, if we listen to God's call, if we spend time fasting and praying to Him, there is no way we can stay the same. God will speak to us, encourage us, guide us, and enable us to live victoriously and to share His message of redemption and covenant to others.

Could we be so dramatically transformed that we would have to wear a veil? I don't know, but what a wonderful problem that would be! I encourage you, dear sister, to climb the mountain of God, fast, and pray for your own breakthrough and transformation. He will answer you.

Today's Prayer:

Dear Lord,

Help me to spend put aside the things and chores of this life in order to spend more time in Your presence. Call me to fast and to pray. Help me to be physically changed by being so close to you, Savior. Help me to act like You, speak like You, and love others like You. Change me Lord. Transform me into Your image. Make me a vessel of shining glory as a holy testament to Your love and salvation!
In Jesus' Name,
Amen

Reflection:

What are your thoughts about today's devotional? What can you do to actively apply these principles?

Dear Sister,

Today I am reminded of the story of Esther. Esther 4:14 asks "Who knoweth whether thou art come to the kingdom for such a time as this?"(KJV). This is an interesting question considering Esther's grass roots. Esther was a young and beautiful Jewish girl living in Persia. Through a string of events that were ordered by the Lord, she found herself in the arms of the king. One minute she was living a simple life and the next thing she knew she was living in a palace, crowned with gold and surrounded by servants. If the story stopped there, people might say, "Look at Queen Esther! She has really made it! The blessings of God are on her! What a success story!"

However, God always has a plan, and His purpose for Esther wasn't her prosperity. Don't get me wrong. I don't think there is anything wrong with Christians being blessed with abundance of land, money, or goods. The Bible is filled with people who were blessed by God. However, God had strategically moved Esther to a position of influence for a greater purpose than just showering His blessings on her. He was going to use her to save His chosen people, and she had no clue of this plan during her rise to fame and fortune. After her Uncle Mordecai told her of evil Haman's plan to commit genocide of the Jews, Esther realized the gravity of her position. Thankfully, Esther made the right choice and found favor in the eyes of the Persian king. He granted her request and the Jews were saved!

What can we modern women glean from this story? Isn't it in the heart of every little girl to grow up, marry a prince, and live happily ever after in a glorious castle? Today's business world is filled with constant striving to get promoted, get a raise, climb the corporate ladder, so when success is achieved, it is easy to focus on the prosperity instead of the purpose that God has for us. If God has moved you into a new position of authority or leadership, ask yourself, "Is there a reason that I am here at this time?" Is there a way that you can use your influence to bless the people of God in your organization or at least stop any discrimination going their way? You may not be preventing genocide, but you might be a vessel used in the Lord's service just in the nick of time to save someone from financial, emotional, or spiritual disaster. Learn from Esther, dear sister, and don't be afraid to use your authority to further God's kingdom.

Today's Prayer:
Dear Lord,

Thank you for blessing me with the position I have today. No matter what job I hold or what limited authority I wield, let me use my position to help Your chosen people. Lord, give me opportunities to bless my Christian brothers and sisters, whether it is food to eat, clothing to wear, money during a financial crisis, a helping hand, or just an encouraging word. Lord, let me hear Your direction for that situation and open a hand of kindness and generosity to Your people. In Jesus' Name,

Amen

Reflection:

What are your thoughts about today's devotional? What can you do to actively apply these principles?

Dear Sister,

       Today I am reminded of the origin of mankind. Genesis 2:7 says "And the Lord God formed man of the dust of the ground, and breathed into his nostrils the breath of life; and man became a living soul" (KJV). This means that all of mankind was created by God from the earth. We are "earthy" creatures! It is no wonder that we love being surrounded by nature.

       I love vacationing at the beach, the mountains, or even by the lake. I am most relaxed when I am around all of God's creation. However, I know that vacations eventually have to end, and I must return to my job. I have to work to earn a living. If we read on in Genesis, we find out a little bit more about our original "nature." Genesis 3:23 says "Therefore the LORD God sent him forth from the garden of Eden, to till the ground from whence he was taken" (KJV). In this same chapter, God curses the ground. As a result of that curse, thorns and thistles came into being.

       After "The Fall of Man," mankind was sentenced to live outside of paradise. As if that weren't enough, because of Adam and Eve's original sin, we have to "till the ground." The word "till" can mean to "cultivate," "work," or "prepare." This is interesting to me because I think it means more than that we must all work to make a living. God says we have to constantly prepare our "ground," the ground from whence we were taken. If God created our flesh from the ground, and we have to prepare our ground, then that means that we are required to "prepare" our flesh. This is the same "ground" or "flesh" that now has thorns and thistles growing in it. In other words, we must actively pull the thorns and thistles out of our ground or flesh.

We all know that we have thorns and thistles in our flesh, and they need to be pulled out! Haven't you ever wondered why we have to keep facing the same obstacles and trials in our lives over and over? It is because we live in a fallen world, and now our flesh is predisposed to sin (i.e. thorns and thistles). We must constantly submit ourselves to the mercy, grace, and salvation of our Lord Jesus Christ. We cannot pull the sin out of our flesh by ourselves. We must call on the ultimate "Master Gardener" to help us! He can supernaturally help us plow our fields, so that we are ready for the harvest. Today, dear Sister, hand over your gardening tools to the Savior, so He can make you bear Godly fruit!

Today's Prayer:

Dear Lord,

I confess that I am an earthy creature and subject to the sins of the flesh. Forgive me for allowing thorns and thistles to grow in my garden. Today, Lord Jesus, I give over control to You. Prune my flesh, so that I can be fruitful and benefit the Kingdom of God. Help my garden be a testament to Your goodness and grace.

In Jesus' Name,

Amen

Reflection:

What are your thoughts about today's devotional? What can you do to actively apply these principles?

Dear Sister,

Today I am reminded of the story of Miriam and Aaron found in Numbers 12. Moses had married an Ethiopian woman, and both Miriam and Aaron didn't like it. They spoke against Moses because of this. In other words, they gossiped. How many of you have listened to or even shared stories about those in leadership? It is easy to criticize people who are leading because they are in the spotlight. All eyes are on them, and every little action they do is scrutinized by people, whether they be good or evil.

Some churches are full of little gossips. Can't you hear them say, "What in the world was she thinking when she chose THAT to wear?" Maybe they might say, "I don't agree with Pastor X's point of view. He is wrong, wrong, wrong!" They might even predict "If she keeps going like that, pretty soon there won't be a congregation left here at all!" No matter what, it is rare that gossips share good news. Usually, they are criticizing the leadership or others in general.

Take heed, Sister, because something shocking happened to Miriam when she spoke against Moses. The Lord came down to the tabernacle in a cloud and called them to Him by name. He chided them about speaking against Moses, His friend, the one whom God spoke to "mouth to mouth" (Num. 12:8 KJV). Can you imagine how frightened they were to be chastised by the Holy One of Israel?! In verse 10, because of her words and heart attitude, Miriam was struck with leprosy. Her entire body was covered by disease, so much so that she looked white from head to toe. She was put outside the camp in solitude for seven days. Then, miraculously, she was healed when Moses pleaded to God on her behalf. The very person Miriam had criticized became her intercessor.

Sister, be careful of your speech because it can spread disease among the body of Christ. Every time someone opens his or her mouth to gossip, it is like spewing leprosy onto the listeners. Then, because it is contagious, the disease spreads and causes pain, hurt, and sometimes spiritual death. Instead of partaking in gossip, intercede for those who would speak ill to others, so that they may be miraculously healed!

Today's Prayer:

Dear Lord,

     Forgive me for taking part in gossip. Heal me from this leprous disease. Help me to guard my mind and my tongue, so that I may bless instead of curse, encourage instead of criticize, and lift up instead of cast down. When I see someone who is speaking ill about Your leaders or others, let me walk away from the situation, and let me intercede for that person, so that he or she may be healed forever! In Jesus' Name,
Amen

Reflection:

    What are your thoughts about today's devotional? What can you do to actively apply these principles?

Dear Sister,

Today I am reminded of the scripture in Numbers 32:23 that says "behold, ye have sinned against the Lord: and be sure your sin will find you out" (KJV). When I was a young girl, we lived in the country. Because my family enjoyed camping so much, my father purchased a camper for the back of his pickup truck. I instantly fell in love with it because it looked like a cute playhouse to me. Everything in it was a bit smaller in size, just right for an eleven year old girl and her little Barbies. However, my father specifically told me not to play in it unless there was an adult home.

One weekend, my best friend came over for a sleep-over. She brought her Barbies too, so we could play all day with them. Dad was working, and Mom had to run into town to get groceries and run errands, so she left us alone for the afternoon. You guessed it. The first thing we did was run out to the camper. It was hot outside, so we cranked all of the windows and vents open, and we played all afternoon in that camper. We had a lot of fun. When it was close to time for Mom to come home, we shut all of the windows and resumed our play in the yard. All went well, and I thought we had pulled it off. Then I heard my father call me to the back porch. He was sitting on the top step, facing the camper. He asked me if I had been in the camper that day. I said earnestly, "Oh no, Daddy. You said not to."

He raised his right hand and pointed at the camper. "Then why is that vent open on the top?" He asked sternly.

I turned around and there, standing tall and proud, like a big white flag saluting my lie, was the top vent that I had forgotten to shut when we left the camper. I immediately knew I was in big trouble. I turned around and confessed right then. "Oh, Daddy! I'm so sorry. I was in the camper today." My face turned red, and I hung my head. He told me to go on upstairs and wait until he took my friend home. She wasn't going to stay the night after all. When he returned, he put a stripe or two across my backside for disobeying him and then lying about it. I learned an important lesson that day.

When we do something that we know God has forbidden, we are acting just like I did back then. Like children, we think we can outsmart God. "I can smoke as long as no one sees it," we might think. Perhaps we take part in something that is immoral or maybe even just improper, thinking that it won't hurt "this once." However, just like my dad did, God sees and knows everything. Nothing is hidden from Him, and we sure can't lie to Him. In the end, we bring punishment upon ourselves. To God, our sins, whether little or big, are just as apparent as that tall, white vent on top of that camper. Learn from my experience, dear Sister, and don't disobey God to begin with.

Today's Prayer,
Dear Lord,

Forgive me for dabbling in sinful activities and thoughts. Help me to keep my mind and body pure by trusting in Your grace and mercy. When sin presents itself to me, help me to be strong enough to turn away and do the right thing. Help me to remember that no act against You is pleasurable enough when compared with Your hand of chastisement. Help me to walk upright in complete integrity, so I can glorify You today.
In Jesus' Name,
Amen

Reflection:

What are your thoughts about today's devotional? What can you do to actively apply these principles?

Dear Sister,

Today I am reminded of how God gave a sign to Gideon, so that he would lead the army of Israel into battle. In Judges 6, we find Gideon struggling with a decision. God had declared that Gideon should lead his people against the Midianites and that Israel would win by Gideon's hand. I can understand why Gideon would hesitate even though an angel had appeared to him with the message. There were thousands of Midianites surrounding the children of Israel, and they were vastly outnumbered. Gideon had to be sure, so he put a fleece before the Lord. He took a sheepskin and put it on the ground overnight. He told the Lord that it would be a sign for him to lead if the fleece were sopping wet from dew in the morning, but the ground would be dry. Sure enough, the fleece was wet and the ground dry. Still, Gideon needed one more sign. He put another fleece out on the ground, but this time he said it would be a sign if the fleece was bone dry and the ground around it saturated with dew. You guessed it. The fleece was dry (Judges 36-40 KJV).

Have you ever needed a sign or assurance from God that you were headed in the right direction? I have. After I rededicated my life to the Lord in my late twenties, I decided that I was going to totally focus on Jesus. I had had very tumultuous and sinful relationships with men throughout my youth, and I wanted to live like a nun, without any distractions from my Godly destiny. I lived like that for seven years. I was following hard after God, growing in His word, and learning all about the leading of the Holy Spirit. One day a friend introduced me to a wonderful, God-fearing, talented man. My friend wanted to play matchmaker, but I didn't want anything to do with it. I didn't want to spend any time pining for a boyfriend, worrying about if or when he would call, playing dress up to impress him. I just wanted to focus on Jesus. However, when I met this man, I knew I was in trouble. I was instantly attracted to him, but when he sat down and began playing the piano, and we started singing in perfect harmony together, I knew he was special. I let down my guard and considered that God may be bringing me a mate. However, the week that followed that meeting was miserable for me. I kept waiting for his call or some indication that he liked me. There were no calls, no notes, nothing.

Finally, I had had enough. I told the Lord, "If this is the man for me, Lord, then let him come to rehearsal tomorrow. If he is not there, then I don't care if he calls me every day or sends a dozen roses every day, I will not give him the time of day or be distracted again. I just can't take it!" I knew that there would be a slim chance of him coming to band practice because he had never joined us before and most likely didn't know what time we met. This was my fleece before the Lord. I needed to know if I should expend my energy on this relationship. The next day, I left for rehearsal early. I reminded the Lord of my fleece along the way, and when I turned into the parking lot, there he was. He was early too, waiting in his truck. As soon as he saw me, he jumped out and ran over to my car. He leaned down and smiled at me through the passenger window, making my heart flutter with his smile. We will celebrate our 21st anniversary this year. Like for Gideon, God was faithful to give me assurance that I was doing the right thing. God wants us to know His will, even if it takes a soggy sheepskin to make it clear to us.

Today's Prayer:
Dear Lord,

Thank You for loving me enough to make Your will clear to me. I need Your direction, Your guidance, and Your presence in my life. Please give me the peace I need to accomplish Your will for my life. Help me to know that I am on the right track. I want to glorify You, Lord, and I want others to see Your light in my life.

In Jesus' Name,

Amen

Reflection:

What are your thoughts about today's devotional? What can you do to actively apply these principles?

Dear Sister,

      Today I am reminded about how important it is for Christians to show kindness to one another. Proverbs 3:27 says "Withhold not good from them to whom it is due, when it is in the power of thine hand to do it" (KJV). I keep this posted in my office as a reminder of the impact a teacher can have on the lives of her students. I know several teachers who have encouraged me when I thought I had no talent, no intelligence, nothing of value to offer this world. These beautiful souls could have chosen not to see the chubby little girl who just wished someone would accept her as she was without judging her appearance. They didn't have to give her a smile or a compliment that lifted her heart, but they did. They took the time to show unexpected kindness to me, and I'm so grateful. Mrs Bayless, my wonderful choir teacher, was the first person who noticed I could sing. I remember how surprised I was when she asked me to compete at state.

      "Me?" I asked with disbelief.

      "Yes, you!" She replied with such enthusiasm that I was forced to think differently about myself.

      Now that I am a teacher, I don't take lightly the mission God has called me to do. Whenever I get the chance, I offer encouragement, direction, and instruction with a side order of God's love. I'm a planter of seeds, one by one, soul by soul. I enjoy watching God give the increase! Look around you, dear sister. Who will be the recipient of your kindness today?

Today's Prayer:

Dear Lord,

    Help me to grow the fruit of kindness in my life. Help me to actively seek out someone who needs to be shown Your kindness through me today. Don't let me withhold any good thing from anyone if I have the power to do so. I submit my will and my attitude to You, so that I won't be distracted by bias or prejudice, but that I will give freely of the kindness that has been shown to me through Your Son, Jesus Christ.

In Jesus' Name,

Amen

Reflection:

What are your thoughts about today's devotional? What can you do to actively apply these principles?

Dear Sister,

There's a chapter in the Bible that's called the love chapter: I Corinthians 13. In it Paul says that he can be the most brilliant man, he can reveal the deep things of the scripture, he can sacrifice his body as a martyr, but if he does any or all of these things and he has no love, then it is worth nothing at all.

Do you know someone who loves to argue? I know people who love to spend hours arguing about miniscule things in the scripture or about small doctrinal things, and they get very heated in their conversations. They get angry. Their faces get red. Their fists curl up into hard balls. What is the purpose of all of this contention? I asked a person that question one time, and he said that the scripture says that we must contend for the faith. I wonder if the scripture that he quoted really meant arguing till the day is long about small jots and tittles of the scripture. I have never seen a single instance where someone came to the saving knowledge of Jesus Christ our Lord by wearing him or her down through heated and exhaustive argument. I've never seen a single arguing match between two individuals where one was suddenly the recipient of Revelation, where he would suddenly after hours of arguing look at the other person and say, "Oh my goodness! I'm wrong and you are right. Now I feel the need to have a deeper walk with Jesus."

I wonder if sometimes the reason why people argue over things in the scripture is because they just like arguing. They like that feeling of winning: that adrenaline rush when they have proved, in their own eyes that they know more than the other person. They derive a selfish and soulish satisfaction from proving that they know that the other person knows that they know all there is to know about that particular element in scripture or particular verse in the Bible. A wise person once told me that "you win your *friends* to Christ."

I wonder how many friendships were deepened or strengthened by even one of these heated arguments that circulate in the church today by supposed scholars of the Bible. Are they arguing because they love God? Are they arguing because they love the other person and truly want him or her to have a deeper relationship with Jesus? I doubt it. I think it is important to know and understand the scriptures. I think that Bible study is an integral part of Christian growth. I just don't think that all of these heated debates are part of a deepening walk with Jesus. I think what we do regarding our study and our interactions with one another should be rooted in love like Paul says. Otherwise, what good are they?

Today's Prayer:

Dear Lord,

    Help me to live the scriptures instead of arguing over them. Help me to be patient and kind when leading others through the Word of God, so that they can have a deeper understanding of Your love and sacrifice for them. Help me to not be distracted by small doctrinal things so much that I forget to love the person You have sent into my life. Help me be a good steward of Your Word and share it with Your love.

In Jesus' Name,

Amen

Reflection:

    What are your thoughts about today's devotional? What can you do to actively apply these principles?

Dear Sister,

When I think about joy and the women of faith in my life, I can't help but think of the story of Dorcas. In the ninth chapter of Acts, we find the story of a lovely, kind-hearted woman, who spent her life serving and giving to others in the city of Joppa. She gave to the poor, and she ministered to the widows in the community. She also was a great seamstress who made many garments as gifts to the women around her.

One day she developed an illness that overtook her, and she died. Peter happened to be there when this happened, and when he arrived, he found all of Dorcus' friends gathered in her home. Each brought with her a garment that Dorcas had made her. They were showing each other how Dorcas had touched their lives, one by one, garment by garment. They were weeping for the loss of this woman, but they were also reflecting and taking comfort in the love that she had shown each of them individually and collectively.

What we do for one another impacts us, more than we realize at the time. To Dorcas, sewing those garments, and giving them to her sisters was just an extension of her care. She clothed them with love, laughter, grace, concern, and attention, not just cloth, and that is what changed those women's lives.

My mother taught me how to cook, can, clean, sew, knit, and crochet from a very young age. Consequently, I love to cook for my guests, especially those who appreciate good southern dishes. I feel a great sense of pride when hearing their groans of pleasure and smacking lips. I also enjoy sewing and crocheting gifts for family and friends. I guess that is another reason why I feel a special connection with Dorcus. I remember sewing Renaissance costumes and head pieces and feeling the thrill when my friends wore them. I remember sewing silly birthday stockings from individually-designed patterns, each based on the particular interest of the recipient. I remember filling them with goodies and watching the joy spreading over my friends' faces and hearing the music of their laughter as they unpacked their stockings. I have crocheted headbands and pillows with 3D flowers, and no telling how many afghans! I cherish the delightful surprise these gifts bring, and I love knowing that my gift is something tangible to remind them of my love for them.

When Peter saw and heard Dorcus' friends, he prayed and God performed a miracle. Dorcus was raised from the dead! What shouts of joy filled that little home that day! Many people heard this story and turned to Christ, so more miracles followed! I love this story because it shows how our laughter and love and care for one another leave permanent marks on our souls. Every time we love each other, we plant a seed for the miraculous! I hope to sow enough joy for a great harvest in heaven!

Today's Prayer:
Dear Lord,

Fill me with Your joy, Lord. Let it bubble up from within me and splash all over those around me. Help me to leave lasting impressions of love, care, and laughter on the hearts and lives of those You send my way. Help me to think of creative ways to leave a legacy of love for my family and friends, so they can take comfort when I am gone. Most of all, Lord, let them remember You and how You have changed me for Your glory.

In Jesus' Name,

Amen

Reflection:

What are your thoughts about today's devotional? What can you do to actively apply these principles?

Dear Sister,

Today I am reminded of the story of Samuel, the Old Testament prophet. This story is found in the third chapter of I Samuel. Samuel was a child who was dedicated to the Lord from birth. He was raised in the temple, and he knew all about religion. He knew how to sacrifice at the altar, trim the candles, add oil to the lamps, and to minister before the Lord. However, he did not KNOW the Lord. When he was sleeping one night, God spoke his name, but Samuel didn't recognize that it was the Lord. God called Samuel four different times that night before Samuel realized that God was calling him out of a life of ritual and into a life of relationship. God was literally giving Samuel a "wake-up call!"

Sometimes I think people hide from God's calling by busying themselves by doing religious things. They figure that they are "doing all right" because they are Sunday school teachers, deacons, church bus drivers, or worship leaders. However, God wants a personal relationship with each person, not just duty-bound service. Have you heard God's voice calling to you into a closer, more intimate relationship with Him? Maybe this is the third or fourth time you have sensed God's invitation. Won't you say what Samuel said when he recognized God's voice? "Speak, Lord, for Thy servant heareth." Samuel's life was changed forever after that, and once you have yielded yourself to God, you will never be the same either

Today's prayer:

Dear Lord,

    I pray that You would wake me up today! I don't want to waste another minute just going through the motions of serving You. I want to hear Your voice and do Your will! Speak to me, Lord, and let me truly hear what You want of me. Change me, oh God, so that I can become more like You. I don't want to stay the same. I want to be transformed by Your will and Your Word today!

In Jesus' Name,

Amen

Reflection:

What are your thoughts about today's devotional? What can you do to actively apply these principles?

Dear Sister,

Today I am reminded of the scripture that says we are one body, fitly joined together. Ephesians 4:16 says, "the whole body fitly joined together and compacted by that which every joint supplieth, according to the effectual working in the measure of every part, maketh increase of the body unto the edifying of itself in love" (KJV).

Have you ever felt out of place, like you just didn't fit in? Remember, dear sister, that in Christ you are perfectly made for the mission God has designed for you, and you have a unique place in the body of Christ. One way to determine your calling is to ask the Holy Spirit to reveal your God-given gifts and desires to you. For example, if God has called you to be a teacher, odds are that you have the rare ability to state concepts in clear ways, so people can easily understand them. If God has called you to be a preacher, odds are that the Holy Scripture burns in your heart, and you are not at peace unless you share the Gospel with others. If God has called you to be a helper, odds are you have the special ability to see what needs to be done before others do, and you take delight in serving others.

Sometimes, though, trouble can arise when people think that one calling is more important or glorious than another. Some may think that preachers, evangelists, or prophets are more important than teachers, servants, or intercessors. However, all are of equal importance to God and His church. As a matter of fact, we NEED each other to survive! I Corinthians 12:21 says, "And the eye cannot say to the hand, 'I have no need of you'; nor again the head to the feet, 'I have no need of you'" (KJV). Should the hand get angry because it is not the eye? Should the foot be angry because it is not the hand? NO! We must rightly discern the body of Christ. We must understand and appreciate all the parts of the body.

Consider this: If the kidney is having trouble in the body, the hand might try to help according to his own calling and say, "your problem is you aren't serving enough! You have to work more and take things into your own hands!" That would make no sense to the kidney, so it would just continue to suffer. However, if another kidney saw what was happening, she might say, "I see the problem. You're having trouble releasing the toxic things from your life. If you let those things go, you and the entire body will feel a lot better!" Because of that wonderful, insightful word of encouragement, that kidney could be healed instead of feeling frustrated or hurt. When we are sensitive to the needs and callings of others, and we operate within our own calling, allowing the gifts of God to work through us, we can bring about healing, and help empower the rest of the body of Christ.

Today's Prayer:

Dear Lord,

    Help me to appreciate the calling of others as they operate within the body of Christ. Even if I don't understand what they are doing, help me to pray for them and encourage them as they travel their own, unique paths with You. Take the spirit of criticism away from me, and help me to speak healing and blessings on them. Never allow me to agree with the enemy regarding another believer, but rather let me agree with the Holy Spirit and say, "God loves you and wants you to follow Him with your whole heart, soul, and mind!" Please give me the words to encourage others to exercise their spiritual gifts within the body of Christ. Help me to embrace my own calling and to be bold to use the gifts You have given me for Your glory and for the empowerment of Your children.

In Jesus' Name,

Amen

Reflection:

    What are your thoughts about today's devotional? What can you do to actively apply these principles?

Dear Sister,

Today I am reminded of when Jesus says "seek ye first the kingdom of God, and His righteousness; and all these things shall be added unto you" (KJV). This scripture is found in Matthew 6:33. Jesus had just given a big list of things that people need for life: food, clothing, shelter. He was talking about everything we need, and we need companionship too.

I had always had bad experiences when it came to relationships with men. My father was an alcoholic who was often verbally abusive and neglectful. When I became old enough to date, I dreamed of falling in love and marrying a good man, but I made poor choices and ended up hurt, angry, and bitter. I used sex to feel accepted and loved, even though true love never really entered the picture. When I came back to Christ, I swore off dating. I didn't want any distractions because I knew I had found true love, the love of Jesus, and I was following Him with my whole heart, soul, and mind. Besides, I felt like I didn't deserve a good, Christian man because of my bad past. Who would want me? I was tarnished goods. How could a good man ever truly love me? However, God had other plans. Just when I thought I had my single life all figured out, He sent me the love of my life: a wonderful, sweet, talented man of God who saw me through the eyes of Christ. He didn't see me as tainted. He saw me as redeemed! It was unbelievable! It turns out that God really does provide everything we need when we seek Him first.

Today's Prayer:

Dear Lord,

      Today I am consciously putting the Kingdom of Heaven first in my life. Help me to keep my eyes on the things You would have me focus on instead of my own selfish desires. Help me to release control to you, Father, and to trust You for all the needs I have to live, love, and prosper for Your glory. Help me to run after You with my whole heart, soul, and mind.

In Jesus' Name,

Amen

Reflection:

What are your thoughts about today's devotional? What can you do to actively apply these principles?

Dear Sister,

Today I am reminded of the scripture that says "He hath shewed thee, O man, what is good; and what doth the LORD require of thee, but to do justly, and to love mercy, and to walk humbly with thy God?" This passage is from Micah 6:8. I love it when the scripture gives us real-life, applicable things to use in our day to day lives. Here, God has boiled things down to the basics for us. We are to focus on three things. We are to concentrate on doing what is just and fair in all our transactions and relationships. his means that we shouldn't cut corners or be sly when it comes to our money. We need to give what we are supposed to give, whether financially or emotionally. We are to live a life filled with mercy, and not just any kind of mercy: God's mercy. In other words, we must remember that no matter how bad someone is, there's a soul inside him or her that Christ died for. We need to respect others because they are recipients of God's grace, just as we are. Lastly, we are to walk humbly before our God, living each day like Jesus is right beside us…because He IS!

Today's Prayer:

Dear Lord,

    Help me to be fair and wise concerning all of my actions today. Help me to be supernaturally objective and not swayed by past behaviors or hurts when making decisions. Lord, help me to be merciful to those around me and to remember that You died for them, as well as for me. I am no better than they are. Lastly, help me to remember that You are with me wherever I go! I can talk to You and ask for Your help and blessing all throughout my day, and You will faithfully answer because You love me.

In Jesus' Name,

Amen

Reflection:

    What are your thoughts about today's devotional? What can you do to actively apply these principles?

FAITH AND MIRACLES

Dear Sister,

Today I am reminded of the scripture regarding the treatment of strangers. Hebrews 13:2 says, "Be not forgetful to entertain strangers: for thereby some have entertained angels unawares" (KJV). I remember when I was in college, and I was living on a very restricted budget. I was renting an efficiency apartment and driving a beat-up old car. I truly was living paycheck to paycheck, and some months, that paycheck seemed to take forever to get to my bank account!

One month, after all of my bills were paid, I had exactly $25 dollars to my name, and that had to last for the rest of the month. That morning, I drove to my early class and came to a stop sign on a side street between two large parking lots. Right as I stopped, a ragged, homeless man crossed in front of my car. I instantly felt the Holy Spirit tell me to give him $20. I couldn't believe it. That would only leave me $5! Surely God didn't want me to give away all of my money. As I drove through the stop sign, I again felt such a strong urge to give him the money that I swerved back around into the parking lot to meet him. I couldn't deny God's will right then, and he jogged over to my car as I rolled down my window. He bent down to eye-level, and I immediately noticed that he was clean-shaven, and had the most amazing clear blue eyes! I held out the $20 and said, "God wants me to give this to you." He smiled broadly, revealing white, even teeth. He thanked me gently, and I rolled my window up and drove around to that same stop sign.

Right then, I realized that I had been so fixated on the money that I had totally forgotten to witness to him! I could have shared the plan of salvation with him, told him that God loved him, or at least offered to pray for him. I turned my car around and zoomed back to the parking lot, but he was gone! It was a very large parking lot, but he was nowhere to be found. He had disappeared! I learned a big lesson that day: don't focus on the money so much that you forget the message. I went on to school, and that afternoon I opened my mailbox to find a refund check for my electricity deposit for $75! No one can convince me that God hadn't used an angel that day to test me and teach me a lesson about giving. Today, dear Sister, when someone asks for help, do what you can because you might be entertaining an angel without knowing it.

Today's Prayer:

Dear Lord,

Open my eyes to needs of others today. Help me to become an abandoned giver. Let me open my hands and give of my time, energy, wisdom, and money to whomever You send across my path. Don't let me turn a cold shoulder to anyone in need. Fill my heart with compassion and generosity today.

In Jesus' Name,

Amen

Reflection:

What are your thoughts about today's devotional? What can you do to actively apply these principles?

Dear Sister,

Today I am reminded of the scripture where God sends Abraham out into the unknown. Genesis 12:1 says "Now the LORD had said unto Abram, Get thee out of thy country, and from thy kindred, and from thy father's house, unto a land that I will shew thee" (KJV). Abraham was new to following God, but when God told him to leave his home and venture out into an unknown land, he obeyed.

Sometimes God asks us to do unusual things to test our faith and often to bless others. This happened to me one Saturday during church visitation. An older sister and I were out visiting the shut-ins and elderly of the church, and we were almost done with our visits when I felt the Holy Spirit prompting me to drive down a specific road. I followed His leading and ended up parking in front of a particular house. I said to my partner, "I believe God wants us to pray for these people today." She looked as surprised as I felt. This was a new experience for both of us. After making sure I was serious, she nodded her head and we walked up to the front door.

After I knocked, a middle-aged woman answered. I introduced us and explained how God had directed us to her door. I said, "I know that you don't know us, but I believe that God sent us here to pray for you today. Is there something specific we can pray with you about?" The woman stared at me with wide eyes; then she excused herself after assuring that we would wait for her return.

She came back to the door with her husband and asked me to

repeat what I had said before, which I did. They exchanged knowing looks, and he shook his head at her and said, "Y'all better come on in."

They explained that they had just heard bad news from their son that very morning. His farm was in deep financial trouble, and they needed a miracle. We held hands in their kitchen and prayed for God to move on their son's behalf and to guide their decisions regarding this issue. They both stated that they knew it was a "God thing" that we showed up on that particular morning. I don't know what happened about the farm, but about two weeks later, the church received a thank you note with a donation, and a testimony of how wonderful it was that God sent them two prayer warriors in their time of need.

Have you ever felt God prompt you to do something new and unexpected, or go somewhere you have never been before? Perhaps he is testing your obedience and wants to use you to bless someone. Dear Sister, listen to Him and follow wherever He leads.

Today's Prayer:

Dear Lord,

Help me be sensitive to Your voice and direction today. Let me be so aware of Your leading that I won't hesitate to do something new, something outside of the box, to bless someone else. Let me be quick to pray for others with faith and compassion. I ask that the gifts of the Holy Spirit be made manifest in me, so that I may glorify Your Holy Name. Let me eagerly take part in Your miracles, healings, and divine directions.

In Jesus' Name,

Amen

Reflection:

What are your thoughts about today's devotional? What can you do to actively apply these principles?

Dear Sister,

      Today I am reminded of the story about Shadrach, Meshach, and Abednego. Chapter three of Daniel is about how King Nebuchadnezzar created a golden image of himself and required that all of Babylon fall to their knees and worship him when they heard the sound of loud music playing. He also decreed that anyone who didn't worship him would be cast into a fiery furnace. All the people in authority came together at the dedication of this image and worshipped the king when the music sounded, all but three Jewish believers named Shadrach, Meshach, and Abednego.

      King Nebuchadnezzar was furious and had them brought before his court. He condemned them to the furnace, but before they left, they said some wonderful, faith-filled words in verses 17 and 18: "Our God whom we serve is able to deliver us from the burning fiery furnace, and he will deliver us out of thine hand, O king. But if not, be it known unto thee, O king, that we will not serve thy gods, nor worship the golden image which thou hast set up" (KJV). This infuriated the king so much that he had the men bound and ordered that the furnace be heated up seven times hotter than normal. It was so hot that the guards who threw the three men into the furnace perished from the heat. However, when the king looked into the furnace, expecting to see his prisoners writhing in pain and burning alive, he saw four men walking around. In addition, he recognized that the fourth man was the Son of God! Jesus was walking around in the fire with the prisoners! The king was astounded and called them to come out of the furnace. When Shadrach, Meshach, and Abednego walked out of the furnace, they were free from bonds and perfectly unharmed. They didn't even smell like smoke! The king became a believer and promoted the three men into places of authority in the kingdom.

This was a test of faith for Shadrach, Meshach, and Abednego. They were getting political pressure to serve another god instead of God Almighty. They were faithful unto death though, and wouldn't back down, even when the king, himself, gave them the ultimatum. Today, being faithful and serving God can bring political "heat" on the heads of believers. They may be asked to behave in ungodly ways just to fit in with what everyone else in the company is doing. Perhaps it is gambling or drinking while on a company trip. Maybe it is taking part in slanderous gossip because someone in authority is exerting pressure to do so. When we don't conform to the world, sometimes others will try to bind us, throw us in the fire, and turn up the heat, waiting to watch us squirm. We must take heart though and continue to serve God faithfully, no matter the consequence.

Just like the three Children of Israel, Jesus will walk through the fire with us, giving us protection and strength. When the trial is over, not only will we rise out of the furnace unharmed, but we will be freed from the very things that bound us in the first place. The enemy wants to kill us, but the very fire he sets for us only serves to burn the ropes that tie our hands and feet. In the end, we will be free, rewarded for our faithfulness, and promoted within the very system that the enemy wanted to destroy us. God is miraculous and takes the plans of the enemy and turns them around to bless God's children.

Today's Prayer:
Dear Lord,

    Help me to be faithful to Your Word and Your will for my life. When I encounter pressure from those around me to turn away from You, give me the strength to say "no." Help me to always have a testimony that is pleasing to you, so that those around me will take note and want You as their Savior too. Help me to take heart and know that You are a miracle worker, a divine protector, and that You love me enough to walk with me through every trial I encounter.
In Jesus' Name,
Amen

Reflection:

    What are your thoughts about today's devotional? What can you do to actively apply these principles?

Dear Sister,

Today I am reminded about how Jesus fed a multitude of people with a few loaves and fish. In John, we find that Jesus had been preaching and performing miracles, so suddenly he and his disciples found themselves surrounded with thousands of hungry people. Jesus wanted to feed them, but the disciples said they had no money to buy food. However, one little boy was willing to share his lunch. John 6:9 says, "There is a lad here who hath five barley loaves and two small fishes, but what are they among so many?" (KJV). Of course, Jesus then supplied the need of every single person there.

Many people concentrate on this miracle when reading this story, but I wonder what we could learn by considering the little boy's perspective. He heard Jesus' call and wanted to help feed the people, but I'm sure he felt his offering was ridiculous in the face of what was needed. However, he gave all that he had anyway. That took courage. That took faith. Jesus responded to that faith with a miracle!

Sometimes we are faced with a great need around us. It may look like the wisdom we have, our limited experience, or even the biblical knowledge we possess is much too small and insignificant to really help. However, we need to remember the faith of that little boy and offer what we do have, so God can perform the miracle. The little boy didn't know how Jesus was going to feed that crowd and neither did the disciples. However, Jesus already knew how to supply such a great need. He was just waiting for someone to come to Him with a little faith offering, so God could be glorified.

Do you need a miracle today? Don't worry about how little you have to give to Jesus, just open your arms and let Jesus have all of your offering. He can take something small and miraculously transform the lives of everyone around you!

Today's prayer:

Dear Lord,

Today I offer all I have to You. Please use me and the gifts within me to make miracles happen! Help me to not limit myself by what I think I can do because You can take the smallest offerings and turn them into something great! Give me the faith and courage to step out in the midst of great need and believe for the best possible outcome!

In Jesus' Name,

Amen

Reflection:

What are your thoughts about today's devotional? What can you do to actively apply these principles?

Dear Sister,

    Today I am reminded of an obscure story found in the Old Testament regarding Elisha and a lost axe head. Have you ever lost something very important, so important that you were almost frantic to find it? Maybe you lost your car keys, the keys to your house, or even a key to your safety deposit box?

    When that happens, your emotions grow very intense, negative, and panic often sets in. Your mind starts to imagine all kinds of sequential repercussions that might happen because of the loss. For example, since you lost your car keys, you won't be able to drive to work. You'll have to call your husband to bring you his set. He will have to leave his job to bring them to you. He might be angry because you lost them in the first place. Maybe you will get written up at your place of employment because you will arrive tardy, all because you lost those keys. How could you do it? How could you lose something so important?! You might start berating yourself and calling yourself "stupid" for losing the item. Wouldn't you like to know a Biblical secret that can help you find things you have lost? This scripture holds an important key for all of us who need help in this area.

    In II Kings, chapter six, we find Elisha and a group of his disciples who are building a camp beside the Jordan River. One of the disciples was cutting a tree near the river, and the axe head he was using fell into the river and sank out of sight. In those days, tools were incredibly important and valuable. They couldn't just run down to the local hardware store and get a replacement like today. This disciple was especially panicked because the axe head wasn't even his to begin with. He had borrowed it. Can you imagine how horrified he would be that he had lost something so precious that someone else had entrusted to him? The disciple immediately sought out Elisha. He told the prophet what had happened. Elisha went to the place where the axe head fell into the river and performed a miracle! He prayed and the axe head floated to the surface of the water, where the disciple was able to retrieve it. There is no physical way that an iron axe head could defy gravity and float to the water's surface except by the power of God!

    When I read this passage many years ago, I felt these words were special. I believe that every word of scripture is written for a purpose, and we are to glean wisdom and direction and promises from God through them. I believe this passage is no exception. Ever since I read this story, I have prayed the "axe head" prayer whenever I lose something. I ask the Lord to supernaturally cause the lost item to rise to the surface of wherever it is, so that I can easily retrieve it. I exercise my faith by praying this, and usually I find the lost item within minutes of praying. Is this magic? Is it witchcraft? No. It is the powerful Word of God in action! Why wouldn't God respond to faith? Why wouldn't God want to help His children find things that are important to them? After all, God specializes in finding lost things. He certainly found me when I was sinking deep in my sins and then redeemed me for His service. He can surely find a missing set of keys!

Today's Prayer:
Dear Lord,

Today, I pray the "axe head" prayer. You are the same yesterday, today, and forever, and Your Word is the same too. The same power that caused that iron axe head to float back during the Old Testament is alive within me today through the Holy Spirit. I pray that wherever my lost item is that You will supernaturally cause it to rise to the surface, so I can retrieve it. When I find this item, I will praise You for Your faithfulness, kindness, and consideration toward Your children. I will give You all the glory that is due.
In Jesus' Name,
Amen

Reflection:

What are your thoughts about today's devotional? What can you do to actively apply these principles

VICTORY

Dear Sister,

    Today I am reminded of the story of the Children of Israel and the quail found in Numbers 11. The Israelites had only been freed from slavery for a few months, and they started complaining about Moses and God. God had been providing manna for them to eat every day, which was a miracle because they were in the wilderness with no other sources of food. Instead of being grateful, the people started longing for the food they ate while they were in captivity. "Remember the fish, cucumbers, onions, and leeks we ate in Egypt?" They said to one another. They cried out for meat and were unsatisfied with what God had given to them. Here they were, fresh from cruel bondage where they had been beaten and subjected to evil dictatorship every day of their lives, yet they were lusting for the things they had before following the Lord.

    At first, when we look at the Children of Israel, we think, "how in the world can they be doing that after all that God has done for them?" However, it is human nature to crave the things of the flesh. How many times do we allow circumstances to take our eyes off Jesus? Before long, we start complaining about the things we don't have or the things that we wish to have? Next, we start to desire things from our old life, from before we were redeemed. It is dangerous to indulge this behavior, dear Sister. Learn from the fate of the Israelites.

God heard their murmurings and cries, and gave them what they wanted: flesh. He sent thousands of quail to their camp, so there would be an overabundance of meat for them. Then verse 33 says, "And while the flesh was yet between their teeth, ere it was chewed, the wrath of the Lord was kindled against the people, and the Lord smote the people" (KJV). Don't let dissatisfaction and lust provoke God's wrath on your life. The lusts of the flesh lead to death. Today, when less than perfect circumstances tempt you to forget the blessings of God, don't cry out for flesh. Instead, cry out for more of Jesus!

Today's prayer:

Dear Lord,

Today I cry out for more of You! Help me to be satisfied with the things of God and not desire the lusts of the flesh or the things of this world. I pray that You would help me to keep my eyes on things that are holy, pure, and good for me. Take the spirit of complaint from me, so that I may speak more freely about the blessings and provision that You have given!

In Jesus' Name,

Amen

Reflection:

What are your thoughts about today's devotional? What can you do to actively apply these principles?

Dear Sister,

    Today I am reminded of God's promise to His children regarding any attack of the enemy. Isaiah 54:17 says that "No weapon that is formed against thee shall prosper" (KJV). The word "formed" could mean "fashioned," "designed," or "twisted." I think that it is interesting that Satan must "form" a weapon in order to come against a child of God.

    When Satan looks at one of God's children, he considers what type of weapon could do the most damage before he fashions it. Satan is not all powerful, like God, so he cannot create anything. He can only twist what is already present. In other words, there has to be some raw materials available in order for him to fashion a weapon. Maybe he sees someone who had an abusive childhood and that is where he begins the formation of his attack. Maybe he finds someone who has a physical limitation or illness, and he takes full advantage of the materials there before he specifically designs a weapon unique to that person's vulnerabilities.

    No matter what our lives hold, it is certain that the enemy wants to twist circumstances, emotions, and events to cause harm. However, we have such a wonderful promise in the Word of God and through the person of Jesus Christ. We now know that the plans of the enemy have no power against us. Satan can try all he wants, but if we submit our minds, bodies, and souls to Christ, there is nothing the enemy can do to harm us. The plans of the enemy cannot prosper or succeed! The next time you feel like your words, deeds, or emotions have been twisted to cause confusion or harm, rebuke the devil in the name of Jesus Christ! Claim this promise and walk with confidence in the full protection and provision of God!

Today's prayer:

Dear Lord,

Today I ask that you reveal the plan of the enemy to me. Help me to release any "material" that the enemy could twist into a weapon against me. Today, I claim my ability to be an overcomer, a conqueror, the victor over my circumstance because of the power of Jesus' blood!

In Jesus' Name,

Amen

Reflection:

What are your thoughts about today's devotional? What can you do to actively apply these principles?

Dear Sister,

    Today I am reminded of when a verse in Proverbs changed both my attitude and my life. Years ago, my husband and I found ourselves living in a second world nation with no vehicle, phone, washer, dryer, and barely any furniture. Tim had been awarded a Fulbright Teacher Exchange. While this was an honor and a great opportunity for him, it definitely presented us with some challenges. Although sometimes foreigners could hire washer-women, there were none to be found for us. While Tim left every morning to teach at the local school, tropical weather, horrible insects, buckets, and a concrete washboard would be my daily companions. It didn't take me long to start feeling sorry for myself. My fingers, hands, and forearms reddened and swelled almost instantly because I wasn't used to that kind of physical labor. I wept from pain every day and prayed that God would send a washer-woman to help me, but none appeared.

    One morning I happened to read Proverbs 31:17: "She girdeth her loins with strength, and strengtheneth her arms" (KJV). Right away, I felt God ask me why I was praying for someone to come do my work for me. I was instantly convicted and encouraged. I had been praying for the wrong thing this entire time! I started praying that God would strengthen my arms, so I could do my own work. Almost immediately, my laundry labor became easier. I started finding a rhythm and pattern to what I was doing, and before long, I began actually taking pride in washing our clothing so well! When the five months were almost over, my husband came home with exciting news. He had finally found a washing woman! I smiled and told him there was now no need because I had become used to the job. It was no problem for me any more. Have you been asking God for someone to do your work for you? Sister, I encourage you to ask God to strengthen you. He is faithful, and He will provide what you need to accomplish the work He has given you.

Today's prayer:

Dear Lord,

    Strengthen me to do the tasks that You have set before me and to not rely on others to do what I should be doing. Help me to stop wallowing in pity and instead rise up and boldly follow You! Help me to set about doing the Father's business in my life. Help me to not be distracted by difficulty, but rather to be invigorated by the challenges You have allowed into my life. Help me to remember that You want what is best for me and will help me overcome any obstacle in my life!

In Jesus' Name,

Amen

Reflection:

    What are your thoughts about today's devotional? What can you do to actively apply these principles?

Dear Sister,

Today I am reminded of the scripture that encourages us to "[cast] down imaginations, and every high thing that exalteth itself against the knowledge of God, and [bring] into captivity every thought to the obedience of Christ"(KJV). This is found in II Corinthians 10:5. The enemy loves to make us doubt the love and provision of God, and he also wants to distract us from our purpose by getting our eyes and thoughts off Jesus and onto ourselves and our circumstances.

We might think, "how can God let this happen to me if He really loves me?" or maybe "I don't deserve to have my needs met or the desires of my heart given to me because I fail so much." However, we possess the power to recognize the ways of the enemy and capture all of those negative thoughts and imaginations. Then we can vocally submit them to Christ by presenting our fears and concerns to Jesus in prayer. In addition, we can conquer those fears and doubts with the powerful Word of God!

The enemy is powerless when faced with Holy Scripture! That is why it is so important to read the Bible and commit scripture to memory. Then when those thoughts try to creep their way into your mind, you can shoot them down with the Truth! Pick a promise, any promise, from the Word of God today and use it to keep the enemy at bay!

Today's Prayer:

Dear Lord,

Today I give you my thoughts and fears. I take every negative and fearful thought captive and submit it to You, Lord Jesus. Your word says that You care for me, and that You are my hope of salvation. I ask you to free my mind from every lie sent from the enemy and every thought of self-doubt, self-loathing, and negativity manufactured by my own flesh. Help me to read and embrace Your Holy Word and actively use it against the enemy of my soul! Thank you for transforming my mind into the mind of Christ.

In Jesus' Name,

Amen

Reflection:

What are your thoughts about today's devotional? What can you do to actively apply these principles?

Dear Sister,

Today I am reminded of the scripture that says, "I will lift up mine eyes unto the hills, from whence cometh my help. My help cometh from the Lord"(KJV). This is found in Psalms 121: 1-2. There are times when things go wrong in life for seemingly no reason at all. It could be a troublesome co-worker who wants to stir up trouble out of spite, or maybe there are sudden, unexpected circumstances that hinder you from the goal you are so close to reaching. At times like these I will try earnestly to correct the situation, doing everything that is within my power to solve the problem, but for some reason, the problem cannot be solved. I have sought information from counseling and self-help books, advice from friends, and other research. All the time, I was looking the enemy in the eye, on a level playing field. Finally, I will remember that God loves me and is waiting for me to turn to Him.

He is the answer to everything. He is far above the battle, looking down from the advantage of His holy mountain. He is well above the enemy and my battle. He has the power. He has the knowledge. He is the ultimate problem solver! Sometimes we look everywhere for help except to the very source that has the solution: Jesus. Today, dear Sister, lift up your eyes and call on Jesus to help you, guide you, inspire you, and refresh you. He is willing and able to provide all you need!

Today's Prayer:

Dear Lord,

Today I lift up my eyes to You, Jesus. I submit my circumstances and troubles to You because You know all things and can see far beyond my limited vision. You are all powerful and can easily defeat those who stand against me. Guide me in the way I should go according to Your perfect will. I give up trying to fix things on my own. I need You, Jesus! I trust that You will supply all the wisdom that I need to live a victorious life for Your glory.

In Jesus' Name,

Amen

Reflection:

What are your thoughts about today's devotional? What can you do to actively apply these principles?

Dear Sister,

Today I am reminded of God's promise to never "fail" us or "forsake" us. This scripture is found in Deuteronomy 31:6: "Be strong and of a good courage, fear not, nor be afraid of them: for the LORD thy God, He it is that doth go with thee; He will not fail thee, nor forsake thee." Moses is encouraging the Children of Israel here, who are about to enter into battle. If you are doing God's work, then you have nothing to fear. No matter what you encounter, God is with you and will never leave you. God cannot be surprised by anything the enemy tries. Therefore, He will never send you into any situation where He doesn't already know the end result. Take heart in that, Sister, because this means there is no pressure on you to win the battle. God already has the victory in His hand. What battle is awaiting your victory shout today?

Today's Prayer:

Dear Lord,

Today I give you my battles. I am stepping out on that battlefield in faith that You will give me the victory! I thank You that You are constantly with me and will never leave my side. In faith, I give a victory shout, "Hallelujah! Get thee behind me, Satan! Victory is mine through Christ Jesus!"

In Jesus' Name,

Amen

Reflection:

What are your thoughts about today's devotional? What can you do to actively apply these principles?

Dear Sister,

Today I am reminded of the scripture that says "Then he said unto them, 'Go your way, eat the fat and drink the sweet, and send portions unto those for whom nothing is prepared, for this day is holy unto our Lord; neither be ye sorry, for the joy of the Lord is your strength'" (KJV). This is from Nehemiah 8:10. I love this scripture because not only does this indicate that we are free to enjoy the wonderful life that God has given us, but that we are to share with others the joy and the provisions that He has given us.

This scripture encourages us to have a joy-filled life and to share that with a lost and dying world. However, it means more to me than that. The second part of that verse empowers us because our joy in God is also what gives us strength. God's joy is a weapon that we can use against the enemy. Hallelujah! When we have a bad day, we can willfully and purposefully exercise that weapon of joy to defeat the plans of the devil. In the end, Satan is under our feet, and that is something to be happy about!

Today's Prayer:

Dear Lord,

    I ask You to release joy into my thoughts, words, and actions. Today, help me to exercise the weapon of joy against the enemy! When coworkers speak against me, let me remember the joy of my salvation. When the world tries to limit me, let me remember that I serve an omnipotent God! When people act hatefully toward me, let me remember that You are in control, so my joy cannot be diminished. Thank You, Lord God, for strengthening me with supernatural joy!

In Jesus' Name,

Amen

Reflection:

    What are your thoughts about today's devotional? What can you do to actively apply these principles?

Dear Sister,

  Today I woke up with a powerful and important scripture on my mind: "And they overcame him by the blood of the Lamb, and by the word of their testimony; and they loved not their lives unto the death"(KJV). This is from Revelation 12:11.

  This passage speaks three things to me. First, we are overcomers or victors because of the blood of Jesus, not because of anything we can do of ourselves. The victory and the glory is because of what Jesus did for us, but we have the assurance that we WILL be victorious no matter what we face! Second, so many of us have suffered or have sinned or have experienced tragedy, but this becomes our testimony because we have survived through Jesus Christ our Lord. It's not enough to just have a testimony though. We must SPEAK our testimony to others. This is part of how we become victorious in our lives. The enemy wants to shame us because of our past, but God wants us to shout out our past because it is a testimony to His saving grace! Lastly, another part of living victoriously is not worrying about our lives or loving our lives more than the call that God has for us. Our lives are not our own, anyway, because they are bought with a price. Dear Sister, I hope you go out of your house today declaring victory by the blood of the Lamb, the word of your testimony, and by putting Jesus first in your life! Amen!

Today's Prayer:

Dear Lord,

Thank You for shedding Your blood to wash away all of my sins. Bring me opportunities to share my testimony with others. Help me to celebrate the victory in my life and how You helped me become an overcomer. I am not ashamed of my past because it proves how wonderful Your grace is. Help me to always put You first in my life.

In Jesus' Name,

Amen

Reflection:

What are your thoughts about today's devotional? What can you do to actively apply these principles?

PEACE

Dear Sister,

Today I am reminded of Moses' personal encounter with the magnificence of God. In Exodus 33, we find Moses on the mountain getting personal instructions from God, and Moses asks to see God's glory. God said it would be too much for Moses to see Him in His fullness, but He would pass by Moses and let him see His "back parts," His Goodness and Mercy (Ex. 33:19-23 KJV).

This exchange between Moses and God has always fascinated me. First, it amazes me that Moses would be so bold as to ask the Almighty to show him His Glory. They had such a wonderful, intimate relationship that Moses felt comfortable asking such a thing. Later, however, I read something in Psalms that gave me a special revelation. In the 23rd Psalm, a very familiar passage for most Christians, I recognized something familiar. It says "Surely goodness and mercy shall follow me all the days of my life" (KJV). Right then, I felt like the Lord wanted me to linger over those words.

We serve a triune God: Father, Son, and Holy Spirit. God made us in His image: body, soul, and spirit. If we are in Christ Jesus, then goodness and mercy MUST follow us because we are made in God's image. If goodness and mercy follow God, then they surely must follow us as well. Another word for "goodness" is "righteousness," and another word for "mercy" is "grace." All of this time righteousness and grace have been following me every day of my life, but I haven't fully realized it. I thought we had to continually SEEK righteousness and grace. However, we are righteous through the shed blood of Jesus Christ, and we have experienced forgiveness and grace because of Jesus' sacrifice. It is a package deal: where ever we go, the righteousness and grace of Christ follow us.

    Now, when I am tempted by the enemy to do or say something that is wrong or sinful, all I have to do is turn back to my constant companion, Righteousness, and say to myself "Nope. I can't do that because of the righteousness of Christ that is with me." Whenever someone tries to tell me that I am not good enough to do something, I can turn to my other traveling buddy, Grace, and say "the Grace of Christ qualifies me to do all things." What wonderful and constant friends God has given us! Dear Sister, let's act like we know the righteousness and grace of God today.

Today's Prayer:

Dear Lord,

    I thank you for sending your Son, Jesus Christ, to save my soul and make me righteous in Your sight. I thank You that You have shed Your Grace on me, and have made me in Your image. Help me to walk this day and every day with the full knowledge of the righteousness and grace You have given me as constant companions for my entire life. Let me become so intimate with You that people will notice something "supernatural" about me when I walk by. Let them sense the goodness and mercy that follow me for Your sake.

In Jesus' Name,

Amen

Reflection:

What are your thoughts about today's devotional? What can you do to actively apply these principles?

Dear Sister,

Today I am reminded of the scripture in John 15, when Jesus is talking about gardening, a subject that is dear to my heart. Verses 5 and 6 say "I am the vine, ye are the branches: He that abideth in me, and I in him, the same bringeth forth much fruit: for without me ye can do nothing. If a man abide not in me, he is cast forth as a branch, and is withered; and men gather them, and cast them into the fire, and they are burned" (KJV). A lot of people focus on the negative aspect of this verse, thinking of it as kind of threatening and works based. They might say "You better get busy and bear some fruit or else you'll be cut off and burned in hell fires." However, this verse isn't about a threat. It's about a promise. Jesus is saying that all who live in Him WILL bear fruit. It is the natural spiritual order of God's law of redemption. There is no guess work about it. If you are redeemed in Christ, you cannot help but bear fruit. If you are saved, the only control you have regarding this is how much fruit you will bear. If you don't want to fulfill your maximum fruit potential, you don't have to, but prepare yourself. God will prune you to produce more fruit. Ouch. Jesus says two things here: No matter what, you are going to bear fruit and you are going be pruned. No one is exempt from God's pruning once in a while.

This verse makes total sense to me from an amateur gardener's perspective. I love to grow tomatoes, squash, and cucumbers. I love preparing the ground, planting, and watching my plants grow throughout the season. I enjoy every stage of this process because it is very satisfying to me to plant something with my own hands and see it all the way through from harvest to the supper table. I will visit my garden daily to water and tend my plants. I provide trellises for my vines to climb, and I trim off all dry, dying leaves or leaves that drag the ground. I know that if they touch the ground, they will pick up pests or disease that might kill the whole plant. I tie up the vines, so they have room to grow and make sure the tomatoes have room to mature.

God is our master gardener. He has to prune the dead and dying stuff out of our lives to keep us healthy. Sometimes He has to separate us from people who might latch onto us and cause us harm or disease. It might not be pleasant, but God doesn't do this to punish us. He does this to protect us, and to keep us healthy, growing, and fruitful. The pruning of God isn't something to be feared, but rather to be embraced as part of God's love and care for us. When God moves people out of our lives or changes our position, then we must be confident that it is not a punishment, but just an indication that we are growing and need more room. Embrace God's hands of direction in your life, dear Sister. It is more proof of his love for you.

Today's Prayer:

Dear Lord,

I submit myself to Your pruning, Lord. Help me to easily let go of the people, places, things, and habits that would prevent me from fulfilling my maximum potential. Lord, let me draw from the strength of the One True Vine, Jesus Christ, and not depend on my own strength of will or talents to gain prestige, fame, or fortune. Instead, let me set my sights on the things of God and Your kingdom. Help me to relax in Your plan, God, and embrace the fruitfulness You have for me.

In Jesus' Name,

Amen

Reflection:

What are your thoughts about today's devotional? What can you do to actively apply these principles?

Dear Sister,

    Today I am reminded of the scripture regarding patience. I first learned about patience in Sunday school. It wasn't that patience was a virtue or even that it preceded wisdom. I learned about patience from the warning of my teacher when she said, "don't pray for patience!" When I asked why, she answered, "because 'tribulation worketh patience!'" She was referring to Romans 5:3-4 which says "but we glory in tribulations also: knowing that tribulation worketh patience; And patience, experience; and experience, hope" (KJV). My first exposure about patience was an admonition not to seek it because I would have to go through a bunch of trials in order to get it. Therefore, I never prayed for it. Not even once.

    Fast forward 45 years, and I'm sitting in a busy, hectic nail salon watching the technician working her magic. She had to work on my hands in between other tasks, and I watched her deftly move between her clients. Out of the blue, she said "You are so patient! I don't know anyone who is as patient as you are!" We laughed about it, but her statement lingered in my thoughts. Me? Patient? If that is true, then how did that happen when I never wanted it or asked God for it? I don't see myself as being patient at all. In my thoughts, I am constantly wishing I were different, better, wiser, more temperate. When I look in the mirror, my giant flaws swell before my eyes. I see rebellion, pride, and lack of compassion. What was that technician seeing that I didn't see?

    Upon prayerful reflection, I realized that patience had entered my life surreptitiously. It seeped in between the trials and the blessings and the prayers over the years. No, I hadn't prayed for it specifically, but God had graciously given it to me a little at a time, as I needed it to live a victorious life through Christ. He gave me a little when I left a career and went back to college, a little when I married the love of my life, a little more when my brother passed away, and more when my father left this earth later that same year.

God continues to gift patience to me as I grow and learn and struggle with my flesh. No, I didn't pray for patience, but neither did I pray for the trials of my life. Nevertheless, both came. We go through tribulations whether we want them or not. It's just part of the mix. Thank God that He gives us what we need and not just what we pray for. Patience? Yes, Lord, I'll take all You wish to give me.

Today's Prayer:

Dear Lord,

    Today, I pray for patience, Lord, because I know You are with me no matter what trials or tribulations come my way. Help me to learn and grow through my trials, so that I can gain experience. With that experience, let me gain hope: hope in Your love, Your grace, Your provision, Your guidance. I give my life over to You completely, Lord. Let my life be filled with all the patience that You wish to gift to me.

In Jesus' Name,

Amen

Reflection:

What are your thoughts about today's devotional? What can you do to actively apply these principles?

Dear Sister,

    When I think about supernatural peace in times of struggle, I always remember the boat story found in Mark 4:39. The story begins with the disciples and Jesus sailing happily across the sea. All is well, and they have been having a great time ministering to the poor, healing the sick, and encouraging the downtrodden. Life was good. They were with Jesus. Miracles abounded. What more could they ask for? Jesus decided to go below and take a nap. Suddenly, there arose a violent storm. It was so bad that the disciples feared for their lives. Now these were sea-faring men who had great experience with what the sea could toss them, but they had never seen a storm so great before. "Where was Jesus?" They asked. He was sleeping peacefully below deck.

    The disciples woke Him up, questioning if He even cared about them. Then Jesus spoke to the storm: "[He] rebuked the wind, and said unto the sea, peace, be still. And the wind ceased, and there was a great calm" (KJV). The storm that the disciples thought would kill them was calmed in an instant, at the sound of Jesus' voice. I think this gives us great insight into human nature and into the supernatural nature of Jesus. Sometimes life seems to be going well, and we are on the top of the world. Then without warning, we enter into a storm in our lives, be it our health, our emotions, our relationships, and/or our minds. The winds of change overpower us, and the waves of doubt and fear relentlessly pummel us. We feel absolutely helpless under this assault. The storm seems so great that we think we are going to die. At the very least, we believe we will become irreversibly damaged. We ask ourselves, "Where is Jesus? He was here a minute ago!"

I have experienced emotional and physical pain so intense that I started to lose hope. I didn't think I could ever recover. However, I kept crying out to God. I held onto Him like the main mast of that ship in the Sea of Galilee, and He heard me. Then, in His perfect time, He supernaturally calmed my fears and helped me to weather that storm, bringing me to a place of safety and into a new understanding of His watch care over me.

We are all on the same ship, sisters. It is a "fellowship." During the storms of our lives, we need to reach out to one another, to encourage one another, to say, "Jesus really cares about you, even now, and He will get you through this! Keep crying out to Him!" We need to hold one another closely, to link arms for strength against the onslaught of waves, to throw out the lifeline that helps us stay connected with Jesus. He is our salvation. He is the one who can speak peace into the storms of our lives. Dear Sister, let's remind each other of that fact!

Today's Prayer:

Dear Lord,

Please help me be the lifeline for someone today. Open my eyes to those around me who are in the middle of a storm. Help me to encourage them, to pray with them and for them, to link arms with them and with You, the author of their salvation. Let me speak the right words that will encourage them to keep going, to keep the faith, to keep trusting in Your care.

In Jesus' Name,

Amen

Reflection:

What are your thoughts about today's devotional? What can you do to actively apply these principles?

Dear Sister,

Today I am reminded of the magnificence of God and His great love for us. In Romans 8:38-39, Paul writes that "neither death, nor life, nor angels, nor principalities, nor powers, nor things present, nor things to come, nor height, nor depth, nor any other creature, shall be able to separate us from the love of God, which is in Christ Jesus our Lord." This is so comforting when we are faced with seemingly insurmountable obstacles, overwhelming fear, debilitating anger, compelling guilt, or our own immeasurable shortcomings.

Sometimes we are our own worst enemy. God has forgiven us, but it is sometimes very hard to forgive ourselves, and even when we believe we have experienced true forgiveness, our minds often wander back during sleepless nights to revisit our many mistakes and feast on them all over again, like some perverse addiction. Dear sister, during these times, remember that God loves you and nothing can keep you from Him! When your mind returns to the memories of your faults, remember this scripture. Reset and refresh your mind with the Word of God and His promises. What can separate us from the love of Christ? Nothing, not even ourselves.

Today's Prayer:

Dear Lord,

I am tired of being my own worst enemy. I need Your help, Jesus! I invite you into my life to help me through my daily struggles and to overcome my failings. I accept Your daily forgiveness and love, and I want You to shine through my life to those surrounding me. Whenever my mind circles back to old thinking habits, I ask that you "reset" it, so I can have the mind of Christ. I accept and depend on Your promises of mercy, rest, and refreshment. Thank you for Your love, Lord Jesus. Help me to truly embrace it every day.

In Jesus' Name,

Amen

Reflection:

What are your thoughts about today's devotional? What can you do to actively apply these principles?

Dear Sister,

Today I am reminded of Paul's writings to the Church at Corinth regarding our inability to understand all that we go through while we are living here on earth. Paul writes, "For now we see through a glass, darkly; but then face to face: now I know in part; but then shall I know even as also I am known" (KJV). This scripture is from II Corinthians 13:12. It is easy to be distracted by how our lives are going right now, dealing with the troubles and concerns that are right before us. It is hard to understand that God has a plan for us that is good when we are going through difficulties right now. I ask myself, "now how can this trial that I am going through ever turn into something good?" I may not understand how, but it can and it does.

I can't begin to tell how many times I have looked back over my life, and I have seen God's hand of protection on me, even though I had to suffer from time to time. Sometimes, though, we won't be able to see what God is up to. We may never truly understand His plan until we get to heaven where all things will be revealed to us. However, right here, right now, we must trust that God loves us and would never allow us to go through something that won't ultimately make us stronger, better, or more mature in Christ. We simply must trust Him and His love for us.

Today's Prayer:

Dear Lord,

      Forgive me for worrying about things I don't understand. Help me to trust You more, God. Thank You for protecting me, healing me, guiding me, and providing everything I need every day. I know You are with me no matter what trials I am facing, and I thank You for Your calming presence in my life. Help me to grow stronger in my faith, Lord. I submit all my cares to You and welcome Your loving embrace.

In Jesus' Name,

Amen

Reflection:

      What are your thoughts about today's devotional? What can you do to actively apply these principles?

Dear Sister,

    Today I am reminded of the scripture that says "For God hath not given us the spirit of fear; but of power, and of love, and of a sound mind." It is from II Timothy 1:7. I rejoice with this scripture because I can claim power, love, and soundness of mind. Jesus has already paid the price for it!

    Sometimes I get in situations where I feel I have no control or power to change anything for the better, like I am a victim of circumstance. However, I can pray with absolute faith that God has given me the victory over whatever I may face before I see the actual physical or emotional victory. Because of this, I can love myself and others without reservation, and I can have peace of mind that God has chosen to give me through the shed blood of Jesus Christ my Lord! Hallelujah!

Today's Prayer:

Dear Lord,

Help me to relax and trust in Your perfect love today. I claim the power of the Holy Spirit along with love and soundness of mind because you have already paid the price for my victory! When obstacles come before me, help me to just breathe and know that You have made me victorious over every single physical or spiritual circumstance before I can even see it. Even when I feel I have no control, help me to remember that You aren't surprised by anything, and You have me covered.

In Jesus' Name,

Amen

Reflection:

What are your thoughts about today's devotional? What can you do to actively apply these principles?

ENCOURAGEMENT

Dear Sister,

Today I am reminded of how God made each and every one of us. Psalm 139:14 says "I will praise thee; for I am fearfully and wonderfully made: marvellous are thy works; and that my soul knoweth right well" (KJV). I often struggle with low self-esteem and sometimes wonder if God really knew what He was doing when He made me the way He did. I feel large, clumsy, unattractive, and rough-edged much of the time. I compare myself with other women who I see as dainty, refined, and walk through life in grace and beauty.

One day I was wallowing in these thoughts while dusting the china in my china hutch. I looked at the shell pink loveliness of one of the cups I was dusting. It was so beautifully made that it seemed translucent. It even had small golden flourishes within the flowers of its design. I complained to the Lord, "why didn't you make me like this china cup, Lord? Instead, I am a big, clunky, ol' coffee mug!" Right away I felt the Lord stop me in my tracks. I knew that I had crossed the line in questioning my perfect and Sovereign Lord. I was in trouble. I felt God ask me a few pointed questions.

"When do you use that china cup?" He asked.

I answered, "Well, only very special occasions, Lord. The china is quite thin, precious, and easy to break. I use it maybe once every few years or so."

"When do you use your coffee mug?" He asked.

"I use my coffee mugs every day, sometimes many times during the day," I replied. "A mug is the first thing I reach for in the morning."

"That is why I made you the way you are. I don't want to keep you on a shelf in a china hutch. I want to use you every day, possibly many times. I want you available for my use at a moment's notice. I may take you on a journey, and you have to be larger and stronger to be able to survive. I may ask you to hold heavy burdens in my service. I may direct you to suffer sudden changes in temperature, based on the challenges I place before you. If you were made like that china cup, you would be broken into pieces before you reach your destination." He continued, "I made you exactly the way you are because I have a purpose for you that only you can accomplish. Don't question the work of MY hands!"

Needless to say, I had to stop and repent for my indulgence in self-pity. I began to praise God for knowing exactly how to design me. Dear Sister, never question God's method or purpose in making you the way you are. Your destiny was determined before you were born. We all have flaws, and we all depend on God's mercy to strengthen, heal, and direct us as we walk down the path of our lives. Aren't you glad that God is the Master Potter and knows the metal He has placed within each of us?

Today's Prayer:

Dear Lord,

    Today I praise you for making me just exactly the way I am. Please use me to the fullest extent today and every day. I praise you that I am fearfully and wonderfully created. My soul rejoices in this knowledge! Help me to not compare myself with others around me, but instead to strive to be like Jesus! I don't want to be kept on a shelf, Lord! Here I am. Use me!

In Jesus' Name,

Amen

Reflection:

    What are your thoughts about today's devotional? What can you do to actively apply these principles?

Dear Sister,

    Today I am reminded of the parable of the unrighteous judge found in Luke 18: 1-8 (KJV). In this passage, we find two interesting characters. One is a judge who is without fear. He doesn't worry about what any person thinks about him, and he doesn't know God at all. God is not part of the mix for him. He doesn't care about religious rules or morals. He makes his determinations based on facts and his own personal sense of justice. The second character in the parable is a widow who has experienced injustice from an "adversary."

    At this time, widows were set apart in Jewish society. They had no husbands to protect them, so they were completely dependent upon others for their livelihoods. She came to the judge and asked to be "avenged" (Luke 18:3 KJV). In other words, she wanted her enemy to be punished for his actions against her. Unfortunately and without any given reason, the judge delayed his judgment. However, the judge eventually relented and gave her justice because of her dogged pursuit and constant petitions. Even though he didn't care about righteousness or about what people thought, he conceded because he was simply tired of her bothering him.

    The scripture ends with an encouraging word. Jesus said that even an unrighteous judge will ultimately provide justice, but God, who is righteous and loves His people, will respond to their needs in a much better way (Luke 18:7 KJV). There is a spiritual principle involved here: the principle of persistence.

We live in a culture of instant gratification, a culture of drive-throughs, microwaves, and Ramen noodles. We want what we want, and we want it now. However, sometimes we must be spiritually persistent and patient to get justice. Sometimes God doesn't immediately rectify our situations. The fact that it takes time to get justice doesn't mean that your argument or situation isn't valid. It just means that God wants you to invest time and effort into your solution or deliverance. Maybe He wants you to spend more fervent time in prayer or subdue your flesh by fasting, or carry out other things that build trust and develop moral character along the way to resolution. No matter what, it is important to keep seeking Him, to keep knocking until you receive your deliverance, your solution, your direction. Don't give up, dear Sister. God has a perfect time table and will answer at the perfect time.

Today's Prayer:
Dear Lord,

You know the needs in my life right now. You know those who have abused me, hurt me, or have dealt unfairly with me. I submit my need for vengeance to Your perfect will right now. Please take control of my mind, will, and emotions, so I can better trust in You and Your perfect timing. I will keep asking You for direction, solution, and deliverance from this situation. I know You love me, and I pray for divine peace while I wait for the full manifestation of Your Will for my life right now.

In Jesus' Name,

Amen

Reflection:

What are your thoughts about today's devotional? What can you do to actively apply these principles?

Dear Sister,

Today I am reminded of how important it is to encourage one another. Mathew 25:37-40 tells us that any time that we minister to each other, it is just like we are helping Jesus. What a wonderful scripture and message about the importance of loving interaction. There have been many desert times in my life. I am one of those people who draws inward when I am going through difficulty. My husband, Tim, is just the opposite. He immediately reaches out to people. His first instinct is to call everyone he knows to ask for prayer. I tease him and say, "Your solution to any problem is to throw people at it!"

I am very different. When faced with illness or mourning, I want to close myself off and deal with things alone. There are merits to each approach, but sometimes God intervenes with the right person at the right time. I'm so grateful that He knows what we need even before we know it.

I remember when I had back surgery at the end of 2012. It was a big deal for me because I was in pain, but I had also never had a major surgery before in my life. Afterwards, I had to rest in bed a lot and severely limit my movements. I felt weak, tired, and grungy. Friends would call, but I wouldn't answer. They then called Tim, but I told him not to let them stop by to visit me. I didn't want anyone to see me in pain, weak, and so disheveled. It was my silly pride, I know. What I didn't know was that I was starting to wander deeper into a desert of despair and depression. I just thought I was going through a healing process, but God knew what would happen to me if I continued this behavior for much longer.

One of my dear friends wouldn't take "no" for an answer. She stopped by, and I could hear her in the living room. I heard Tim tell her that I was resting, and I heard her start walking down the hall toward me. She said, "I just want to say hi to her." The next thing I knew, she was standing next to my bed, looking down at me. She placed her hand on my arm and told me how much she loved me. I didn't see anything in her eyes but mercy and acceptance. I started crying immediately. I realized right then that I was holding onto a lot of fear and anxiety that had been building up since before the surgery. Her visit "allowed" me to let go and release all of it. God knew what I really needed was a sister's hand to pull me out of my desert of fear.

I think one way we can help each other is to sensitively follow the leading of the Holy Spirit, even against another person's wishes. Ultimately, God knows what we need more than we do.

Today's Prayer:

Dear Lord,

Help me to be sensitive to Your Holy Spirit. Place me where I can hold out a cup a water to someone who is thirsty, clothe someone who is wearing rags, visit someone who is ill or in prison. Let me see them through Your eyes, Lord. Let me encourage my sisters with loving words and gentle hugs. Use me, Lord, to bless Your children today.

In Jesus' Name,

Amen

Reflection:

What are your thoughts about today's devotional? What can you do to actively apply these principles?

Dear Sister,

    Today I am reminded of when Paul encouraged the Philippian church to pay close attention to their thought lives. He said "whatsoever things are true, whatsoever things are honest, whatsoever things are just, whatsoever things are pure, whatsoever things are lovely, whatsoever things are of good report; if there be any virtue, and if there be any praise, think on these things." This is found in Philippians 4:8.

    Every day we are saturated with negativity. The news is filled with disasters, crimes, epidemics, and political corruption. The movies we watch are teeming with depravity, despair, and cruelty. The music we listen to promotes poor moral choices and instant gratification. We work with some people who don't understand or value kindness and charity. If ever there was a time for us to lift up our eyes toward heaven and cry out for help, it is now. However, even though there is so much loss and despair in the world, we have hope in Christ.

    I have found that when I am actively looking for them, the Lord will bring true, honest, just, pure, lovely things into my path. If I consciously focus on those things, then my attitude automatically changes for the better. If we spend our time thinking of these good things, then it is just that much easier for us to actively spread the goodness, kindness, and grace of God to others. That is just the way God made us.

Today's Prayer:

Dear Lord,

Help me to meditate on all of the good things that surround me today. I pray that You will give me the spiritual eyes to see what is true, honest, and lovely as I go through my daily routine. Help me to capture any negative thoughts and cast them at the feet of Jesus, so I can focus on bringing more kindness and grace to those who are around me.

In Jesus' Name,

Amen

Reflection:

What are your thoughts about today's devotional? What can you do to actively apply these principles?

EVANGELISM

Dear Sister,

Today I am reminded of Paul's encouraging word to the Philippian Church: "I press toward the mark for the prize of the high calling of God in Christ Jesus" (KJV). This is found in Philippians 3:14. The calling of the Lord is powerful and compelling. Certainly, it was very dramatic when Jesus called Paul into the ministry. However, even Paul (whose name was Saul at that time) didn't fully embrace the call right away. He had to go three days of complete physical blindness before Jesus became real to him.

I think we all have to get to a point where Jesus is so real to us that we HAVE to follow Him. We simply couldn't be satisfied unless we did. As a young Christian, around the age of twelve, I was taught about many restrictions for women regarding service to the Lord. As a result, I didn't think women were allowed to preach or teach to the entire church from the pulpit. I thought it was only appropriate if women taught other women, young children in Sunday School or served as secretaries or in other positions without authority. However, I found out that God will often call women into full-time ministry by way of personal revelation.

When I returned to the Lord as an adult, our church had a guest speaker, and after a wonderful message, he asked for people who wanted prayer to come to the altar. I moved forward and stood, patiently waiting for him to pray for me. When he reached me, he simply touched my face and I fell to the ground. I immediately felt calm, quiet, and peaceful. My eyes were closed, but I could see reds, golds, and yellows flowing back and forth beneath my eyelids.

Then I heard it: a deep, loving, assuring voice that said "You are called. You are anointed. You are my minister." I didn't question it because of the peace I felt all throughout my being. I don't know how long I was on the floor, but when I opened my eyes, everyone but the preacher and a couple dear friends were gone. When I told my pastor what I heard, he smiled and said that God was calling me into His service. The calling of Jesus is the prize I press toward now. I'm not limited by what anyone else thinks. God's calling is a high calling, and it is as challenging as it is rewarding, but I want to finish this race with strength! What is God calling you to do?

Today's Prayer:

Dear Lord,

Open my heart and mind, so I can hear You calling me. I will go where You want me to go and do what You want me to do, even if my family and friends don't understand it. Let me trust You more than social conventions. Let me follow Your Holy Spirit in all things, and help me to grow in word and deed according to Your will.

In Jesus' Name,

Amen

Reflection:

What are your thoughts about today's devotional? What can you do to actively apply these principles?

Dear Sister,

    Today I am reminded of the scripture in II Corinthians 3:3 that says "ye are manifestly declared to be the epistle of Christ ministered by us, written not with ink, but with the Spirit of the living God; not in tables of stone, but in fleshy tables of the heart" (KJV). We are epistles of Christ. An epistle is a means of communication. It is a letter sent from one person to another or to a group of people. Here, Paul says that we are "manifestly" or "clearly" physical representatives of the spiritual communication of Christ. This means that we are constantly sending a message to those around us about Jesus even if we aren't opening our mouths. Just our physical presence is enough for others to notice that there is just something different about us. The way we act, treat our friends, families, acquaintances, waitresses, and even sales clerks lets people know about God. Our speech and behavior is different because of Christ within us.

    Sometimes we are aware we are being "read," and other times we never know. For example, I was visiting with a coworker the other day. I was just passing the time with her, sharing something that I had done over the weekend. The next day, she mentioned that she had been thinking about our conversation and something spiritual I had said that was confirmed by her daily devotional that morning. She was blessed by our discussion, but I was totally unaware that God had been using me at that time. I had no more control over her "reading" me than if I were a book on a library shelf. I'm glad that the message she received was one of blessing. If we truly are books of Christ, then "whosoever will" can read us. Sister, what message are you sending about Jesus today?

Today's Prayer:

Dear Lord,

    Help me to be a "good read" from someone who needs a spiritual "self-help" book. Let him or her see Jesus' goodness and mercy within my pages. Fill my mouth with Your words, Lord, so that I can be a blessing to those around me, whether I know they are listening or not. Help me to reflect the Light of Christ no matter who "reads" me today and every day.

In Jesus' Name,

Amen

Reflection:

    What are your thoughts about today's devotional? What can you do to actively apply these principles?

Dear Sister,

    Today I am reminded of the passage in Luke 24 that describes how Jesus appeared to the disciples after His resurrection. The disciples were gathered together as usual, and suddenly Jesus appeared right in the middle of them. Can you imagine how surprised they were? They thought they were hallucinating and couldn't believe it really was the Lord, even when they saw His hands and feet. Then Jesus asks for something to eat. They gave him some fish and honeycomb and watched as Jesus ate it in front of them. He did this to prove that He wasn't a spirit, but was flesh and blood. Even then, they really couldn't comprehend that the Lord really was with them again. Isn't this a perfect example of the limitations that people put on God? I wonder how many times that Jesus has been walking beside us and we don't notice or believe that He really is with us? The disciples were seeing Him with their own eyes, yet couldn't really understand how it could be Him.

    Then Jesus does something very interesting. Verse 45 says "Then opened He their understanding, that they might understand the scriptures" (KJV). Jesus supernaturally opens the minds of the disciples to enable them to believe beyond their own understanding. What a beautiful act of love. God wants us to know Him and to understand His Word. Have you ever read a scripture over and over without really thinking it was special, but then one day, something is different, and suddenly that same scripture becomes alive with meaning for you? Guess what? That means that God supernaturally opened your mind to understand His Word because it was necessary for you to fully comprehend it within God's perfect time frame for your life.

It is so important to ask Jesus to reveal Himself to us through the Holy Bible. He is faithful, and He will allow you to view His truth beyond the limitations of your physical mind. This passage goes on to explain that Jesus opened their minds because He wanted them to be witnesses of His resurrection and the salvation He offers to all who call on His name. This means that we need to follow through when God gives us personal revelation in His word. God wants us to witness to others and share what we have read, seen, and experienced in our lives. It is not enough to just "sit" on God's Word. God wants us to take action and share His redemption story!

Today's Prayer:
Dear Lord,

I pray that when I read Your Word, that you will open my mind to truly understand the messages You have for my life. Help me not to limit the work You are doing in my mind, body, and spirit, but to truly embrace my transformation as Your servant. I want to know You, Lord. I want to understand Your precepts and ways. Help me to be a powerful witness for Your glory and to share my experiences and revelations, so that others can come to know You as their Lord and Savior.

In Jesus' Name,
Amen

Reflection:

What are your thoughts about today's devotional? What can you do to actively apply these principles?

Dear Sister,

    Today I am reminded of how John the Baptist was introduced in John 1:23: "[John] said, I am the voice of one crying in the wilderness, Make straight the way of the Lord" (KJV). Even though this was written over 2000 years ago, it is still true today. We may not be wandering in a desert, but we go out into a jungle every day of our lives. There are things in our modern wilderness that are every bit as dangerous as if we were journeying into the heart of the Amazon.

    Our modern world is filled with drugs, pollution, grief, sickness, and violence. If ever there was a time when we needed to cry out to others about the way of God, this is it! Every day, we come in contact with people who are drowning for lack of hope and direction. We need to let our light shine in the wilderness. We need to cry out to those around us, to show them the way to hope, victory, healing: Jesus!

Today's Prayer:

Dear Lord,

    Help me to be like John the Baptist and cry out that You are the Way, the Truth, and the Life to all those around me. Help me to shine with the light of the Holy Ghost and point the way to salvation. Help me to see those who need healing and tell them that You are their healer. Help me to see those who are struggling with addiction and show them the way to victory through Jesus Christ. Help me to see those who are feeling hopeless and give them words of encouragement! Lord, I devote this day to leading others to You.

In Jesus' Name,

Amen

Reflection:

    What are your thoughts about today's devotional? What can you do to actively apply these principles?

Dear Sister,

Today I am reminded of the story of Lazarus. He had died and had been buried in a tomb for four days. Then Jesus called him forth by name. "And he that was dead came forth, bound hand and foot with grave clothes: and his face was bound about with a napkin. Jesus saith unto them, 'Loose him, and let him go'" (KJV). This is from John 11:44.

Most people concentrate on the miracle of resurrection when they read this scripture, and that certainly is wonderful. However, what I found interesting about this is that although Lazarus was healed and resurrected, his body and face were still bound by grave clothes. He was resurrected, but he was still limited by the things that had put him in the grave to begin with. Interestingly, the first thing Jesus did was command that His followers go forward and release Lazarus. In other words, it is our joyful mission to help release those who are newly saved by grace from the things of the world, the things that keep them "bound" up! Praise God! We are also required to help remove the obstacles that would keep them from seeing the world through their new eyes in Christ. How do we do this? We do this by getting involved and putting our hands of kindness and guidance on them and their lives, by stepping outside ourselves to help others. Dear Sister, who can you help today?

Today's Prayer:

Dear Lord,

    Bring me into the path of new believers today, so I may help them on the newly chosen way. Fill my mind and mouth with words of wisdom, encouragement, and Godly advice, so that their grave clothes will fall away from them and not hinder them anymore! Give me eyes to see what needs to be done to help others today, and help me to lead with an example of kindness and not judgement.

In Jesus' Name,

Amen

Reflection:

    What are your thoughts about today's devotional? What can you do to actively apply these principles?

Dear Sister,

     Today I am reminded of the story about the woman at the well. She had a divine encounter with Jesus and learned first-hand about the living water He offered. As soon as she became saved, she ran into town to tell all who would listen. "The woman then left her water pot, and went her way into the city and said to the men, 'Come, see a man who told me all things that ever I did. Is not this the Christ?' Then they went out of the city and came unto Him"(KJV). This is from John 4:28-30.

     This scripture touches me because I was like that woman at the well, trying to quench a thirst with all the things that the world had to offer me. I started drinking from the well of religion when I was young, but found no satisfaction in "doing my duty" or just going through rituals without a relationship with Christ. Then I decided that I would try the well of the world for most of my young adulthood. I fooled myself into thinking that I was drawing happiness from that well, but I was never satisfied. Then I met Jesus, and I found out that I didn't need religion. I didn't need the world. I needed a savior. When I started walking with Him, I was filled with true joy. I can totally understand why the woman at the well couldn't remain silent. She had found the secret to true joy! Which well will you choose, dear Sister?

Today's Prayer:

Dear Lord,

Thank you for leading me to the well of salvation. Help me to be like the woman at the well and bring others to Your well of everlasting life. Help me to find my happiness in the things of God and not the things of the world. Help me to splash the water of joy over all those who cross my path, so that they may know what a wonderful Savior You are.

In Jesus' Name,

Amen

Reflection:

What are your thoughts about today's devotional? What can you do to actively apply these principles?

FORGIVENESS

Dear Sister,

    Today I am reminded of Jesus's words about forgiveness. In Matthew 18: 21-22, Peter presents a scenario where a brother sins against him repeatedly, and then he asks Jesus how many times he should forgive him. Peter suggests seven times, and Jesus said not just seven times, but "seventy times seven" (KJV). If you do the math, that equals 490. This seems extreme because who would let someone sin against him or her so many times? Furthermore, what transgressor would ask forgiveness hundreds of times?

    At first this may sound silly, but when you think about human nature, it makes more sense. For example, have you ever been hurt and then forgave the person who hurt you? Then months later, maybe when you are lying awake in the middle of the night, you remember what that person did and begin to stew about it over and over, reliving the incident? Suddenly all of those negative emotions overwhelm you, and you find yourself angry with that person all over again. Here is a good time to actively and purposefully forgive. We must choose to forgive again and again, every time those thoughts try to enter our minds and hearts. We don't forgive because the person asks or deserves it, but because unforgiveness has an unholy root. It will continue to grow in our lives if we don't pull it out.

    Unforgiveness is like a weed in our garden. If we don't pluck out that weed of bitterness and hurt, it will sprout all over again, even though the actual act was long ago and the person may not even still be in our lives. Jesus knows how our minds can work against us, and His spiritual direction can free us from a life filled with bitter disappointment. Dear Sister, if you struggle with hurtful memories, then take this verse to heart and ask Jesus to help you forgive. Remember that Jesus forgave you when you didn't deserve it, so this is your turn to act like Jesus and forgive, even if it takes 490 times to get the job done.

Today's prayer:

Dear Lord,

   Help me to forgive those who have knowingly or unknowingly hurt me. Whenever the enemy tries to bring those hurtful actions back into my mind, help me to speak out loud, "I forgive her" every single time. Then help me to speak blessings and peace over that person. Help me to live a life free of unforgiveness and to walk in the full love of Christ.

In Jesus' Name,

Amen

Reflection:

   What are your thoughts about today's devotional? What can you do to actively apply these principles?

Dear Sister,

    Today I am reminded of the scripture that says "If the Son therefore shall make you free, ye shall be free indeed" (KJV). This scripture is found in John 8:36. Before I had a real relationship with Jesus, I used to pity Christians. I thought they were slaves to a God of judgment, a God who was always ready with a whip in one hand and a book of rules in the other. I wanted to LIVE. I wanted to be FREE.

    However, after living on my own for years and doing everything that I was taught not to do, I had a revelation about my life and came back to Christ. Then I was able to look back on my life without fleshly blinders on. What did I miss from my old life? What freedom was I giving up? Was it the unending partying or all the subsequent hangovers? Was it the drug-induced paranoia or the worry about an unwanted pregnancy? Was it all the guilt and all the lying? What kind of freedom was that? What kind of living was that?

    Now I know I was deceived by my own fleshly desires and the enemy of Christ. Now I want to serve Him because He saved me, not because I had to earn His favor or love. I am not forced to do anything for Him. I live for Him because I love him. Jesus has truly set me free: freedom from guilt, shame, deceit, and worry. Now I love my life because I am free indeed!

Today's Prayer:

Dear Lord,

Thank You for saving my soul and setting my feet on the path of righteousness. Thank You for delivering me from the enemy's traps and snares. Thank You for freeing my soul and filling my heart with love, peace, and joy. Thank You for providing a way for me to live in total freedom from guilt and shame. Today, I willingly choose to serve You and follow Your commandments.

In Jesus' Name,

Amen

Reflection:

What are your thoughts about today's devotional? What can you do to actively apply these principles?

Dear Sister,

Today I am reminded of the story of the waters of Marah. The children of Israel were thirsty and came upon some water, but it wasn't fit to drink because it was bitter. Then Moses "cried unto the LORD; and the LORD shewed him a tree, which when he had cast into the waters, the waters were made sweet." This scripture is from Exodus 15:25. I love this scripture because it is a foreshadowing of the sweetness from the tree of Calvary.

Before I knew Jesus, I was just like the pool at Marah. I was bitter and no good to anyone, least of all myself. I was bitter about life, love, and people. However, when Jesus came into my life and touched me with His cross, the waters within me became sweet and I began to see people through the eyes of Christ. No matter what your past has been, Dear Sister, Christ has given you the sweet water of salvation, and you will never thirst again. What sweet water it is!

Today's Prayer:

Dear Lord,

      Thank You for Your transforming mercy. You took my bitter heart and filled it with Your sweet goodness and salvation! Help me to put my sinful past behind me and to revel in the sweet waters of Your purpose for my new life. Help me to see others through Your eyes, Jesus. Let me be the one to lead them to Your everlasting pool to quench their thirsty souls!

In Jesus' Name,

Amen

Reflection:

    What are your thoughts about today's devotional? What can you do to actively apply these principles?

ABOUT THE AUTHOR

Dr. Marla Bennett is a Jesus follower and a college professor. She is a teacher, writer, poet, praise and worship leader, and motivational speaker. She holds a doctorate of Educational Leadership, a Specialist degree in Community College Teaching, and a Master's degree in English. She is a creative writer who has won many state-wide honors for her poetry.

Made in the USA
Monee, IL
26 January 2020